AMERICAN AVIATION
The First Half-Century

David Willis
with Richard James Molloy, Jim Winchester, and Sean Clark

Published by Key Books
An imprint of Key Publishing Ltd
PO Box 100
Stamford
Lincs PE9 1XQ

www.keypublishing.com

ISBN 978 1 80282 303 5

Typeset by SJmagic DESIGN SERVICES, India.

CONTENTS

Aviation and showmanship were intimately linked in the United States during the first half of the 20th century – from the exhibitions of the pioneering age, to the barnstorming and record breaking of the 1920s and 1930s, and on after the war. Here, Bruce Parker rides the waves in Biscayne Bay in Miami, Florida, in 1946, with the help of a Luscombe 8. To Americans that come of age during the 1930s and 1940s, Parker was "Mr. Water Skiing." He became the first overall champion at the inaugural National Water Ski event at Jones Beach on Long Island, New York, in 1939, performed at water shows, taught others the skills required at his schools and participated in many stunts. The Luscombe 8 went on to become one of the most successful American light aircraft.

AUTHOR'S NOTE
AMERICAN WINGS

In early 2022, I was approached to put together a companion volume to the earlier *British Aviation: The First Half-Century*. Like its predecessor, the idea was to take black and white images and add color. It would cover aircraft built in the United States up to 1950.

My first thought (with apologies to Roy Scheider) was "You're gonna need a bigger book." The number of aircraft types built in the first half of the 20th century in the United States is high. A quick flick through Joseph P. Juptner's wonderful nine-volume *US Civil Aircraft* series gave an indication of the breadth of commercial aircraft that could be included. Ten minutes with John M. Andrade's *U.S. Military Aircraft Designations and Serials 1909 to 1979* highlighted the diversity of warplanes produced in the country by 1950. I quickly concluded that filling 192 pages would not be a problem.

But providing adequate coverage for each of the five decades might be. As with the earlier volume, I wanted to portray as wide a diversity of aircraft as possible, a mix of the well-known and obscure, the great and the not-so-great. The problem, as I saw it, is that information for certain periods of American aviation is thin on the ground, especially for someone living to the east of the Atlantic Ocean. While huge numbers of articles and books are available on US aircraft of the World Wars, the more successful airliners and the most popular sports aircraft, finding reliable information on (for example) American military aircraft prior to 1917 is more time consuming.

The solution was to share the writing and research duties. Jim Winchester was kind enough to take on the role of compiling the captions for several sections of this volume. Without his participation in this project, it would have taken far longer and be much the poorer.

At its core, this is a book of images. Responsibility for breathing new life into old pictures rested with Richard Molloy and Sean Clark. From a pile of black and white photos, many in poor condition, they produced the beautiful artwork that is at the heart of this book. Determining colors from black and white images is a notoriously difficult task; in many cases, little or no reference material is available and, as it was my task to search it out, any mistakes that have made it onto the page are mine.

Other people also helped to make this project a reality. Chief among them were Brianne Bellio and Anita Baker of Key Publishing, with the former assuming the role of project manager for this book. My thanks also go to those that produced the references I used in putting this volume together. Not just Juptner and Andrade, but the authors of the other books, articles, and websites that were consulted. While too numerous to list, without their work, this project would have been impossible.

David Willis
Wittering, September 2022

AMERICAN AVIATION
THE FIRST HALF-CENTURY

Great Oaks from Little Acorns Grow

The first five decades of the 20th century were a tumultuous time for aviation. In 1900, no one had flown a powered heavier-than-air aircraft; by 1950, millions of people had traveled and, during two world wars, fought, in the air.

From initial hops barely faster than a horse could gallop, by the end of the half-century an aircraft had flown nonstop to Ohio from Perth in Australia – 11,236 miles (18,083km) – while the "sound barrier" had been broken. These milestones, the former of which was achieved by Commanders Eugene P. Rankin, Thomas D. Davies and Walter S. Reid, and Lieutenant Commander Roy H. Tabeling of the US Navy, flying a Lockheed P2V-1 Neptune, and the latter by Captain Charles "Chuck" Yeager of the US Air Force in the Bell X-1 rocket-powered aircraft, occurred in September 1946 and October 1947, respectively, soon after the end of World War Two.

By 1950, over half a million Americans were certified pilots and a further 281,800 of their fellow citizens earned their living within the aviation manufacturing industry, turning out a diverse range of flying machines for both military and commercial use. Just under 6,300 aircraft were built in the United States that year, and while this was a fraction of the number assembled in the country between 1940 and 1945, the start of the Korean War in June 1950 triggered a surge in military orders in the years to come.

Aviation was an integral part of American life by 1950. Reaching that point, however, was a long and, at times, difficult road. Tempting as it is to point to the first flight by a powered, heavier-than-air machine as the start of it all, the seeds of American aviation were planted earlier, in the last decades of the 19th century.

First Steps

John Joseph Montgomery is understood to have made the first controlled flight by a heavier-than-air flying machine in America. He built and tested a series of gliders from 1883 at Otay Mesa, near San Diego in California. He never publicized the flights at the time, revealing them at the Aeronautical Congress Conference on Aerial Navigation at Chicago between August 1 and 4, 1893. A physicist and engineer, he later worked at Santa Clara University, where he became a professor in 1901.

Montgomery originally experimented with three ornithopter designs, before correctly concluding that human strength was insufficient to power such machines. He turned his attention to fixed-wing gliders, initially building free-flying scale models before progressing to the first of three man-carrying gliders constructed between 1883 and 1886. Montgomery paid particular attention to the airfoils he used and different methods of control.

The first flew on August 28, 1883, and became the most successful of the three in terms of distance flown, eventually flying around 600ft (183m) in the spring of 1884. The second incorporated hinged flaps on the trailing edge of its flat airfoil, to alleviate sensitivity to gusts and provide roll control, and considerable dihedral for stability. The third had a "parabolically" (cambered) airfoil and the angle of incidence could be varied independently or in unison. The last two gliders proved disappointing in terms of gliding distance, leading him to investigate the aerodynamics of airfoils.

From 1904, Montgomery tested the *Montgomery Aeroplane* (later renamed *The Santa Clara*), a tandem wing glider. In March 1905, he was carried aloft in the aircraft by a balloon, gliding to the ground after release, and then built another glider known as *The California*. Tests came to an end after the massive earthquake that struck California on April 18, 1906, and Montgomery did not resume his gliding experiments until 1911 at a camp south of San Jose at Evergreen, after which he named his new machine. The *Evergreen* had a new control system, with pitch and roll controlled by warping (twisting) the wings. He was killed while landing the *Evergreen* on October 31, 1911.

The Father of Aeronautics

Montgomery was invited to lecture at the Chicago congress by its chairs, Octave Alexandré Chanute and Albert Francis Zahm. Chanute can rightly be considered the "father" of heavier-than-air flight. He made substantial contributions to aeronautics, including devising the strut-wire-braced wing structure used by biplanes, and building a series of man-carrying gliders between 1894 and 1904, assisted by Augustus Moore Herring and William Avery. Of equal importance was his role as a compiler of aeronautical developments, and his willingness to dispense advice to others working in the field. In effect, he acted as a central source of information, communicating with and helping many of the leading pioneers of "aviation" – a term he popularized – during its infancy.

French-born Chanute had a successful career as a civil engineer before turning his attention, full time, to solving the problems of manned flight in 1889. He began by gathering and cataloging the work of others, analyzing what worked and what did not, and publishing his results in a series of articles from 1891. They were compiled within the book *Progress in Flying Machines* in 1894.

Aerodrome

Several important events occurred in 1896. That year, Chanute tested three gliders at Miller Beech in Gary, Indiana, along the shore of the southern tip of Lake Michigan. During one series of experiments conducted in August and September, Herring flew a biplane design for up to 14 seconds, covering a maximum of 359ft (109m). The potential dangers of flight were also highlighted that year. On August 10, the German pioneer Otto Lilienthal died from his injuries after crashing his glider the previous day.

Two months earlier, a steam-powered tandem-wing flying machine managed to fly for 3,300ft (1,006m), ten times further than earlier heavier-than-air creations. Designed by Samuel Pierpont Langley, the third Secretary of the Smithsonian Institute, his "Number 5" was a 25lb (11kg) machine launched via a catapult from a houseboat on the Potomac River near Quantico, Virginia. On November 11, the "Number 6" increased the distance flown to 5,000ft (1,524m).

In 1898, based on the success of his models, Langley received grants of US$50,000 from the US Department of War and US$20,000 from the Smithsonian – huge sums of money for the time – to develop a full-scale piloted version, which he named "Aerodrome," also retrospectively applied to his smaller models. The design was to be inherently stable, as were his scale models, so only a primitive control system was needed, leaving the pilot with the task of pointing it in the right direction. Stephen Marius Balzer was contracted to produce an internal combustion engine for the Aerodrome, while Charles Matthews Manly was hired as an engineer, although, along with others, he later played a role perfecting the 52hp (39kW) radial engine.

Development of the Aerodrome was protracted and ultimately unsuccessful. An unmanned quarter-scale model flew twice with a gasoline-powered engine on June 18, 1901, and again on August 8, 1903. The full-size machine was rather less successful, however. With Manly at the controls, it was catapulted from the houseboat on October 7, 1903, but failed to reach sufficient speed for flight and descended into the Potomac. A second try on December 8 ended the same way. Although blaming the launch mechanism, Langley made no further attempts to fly the Aerodrome.

Control is the Key

Nine days after Manly was rescued from the Potomac for a second time, two brothers from Dayton in Ohio made the first sustained and controlled flight in a powered, heavier-than-air flying machine. Orville and Wilbur Wright, owners of the Wright Cycle Company, began investigating the possibility of manned flight in 1896, having followed the progress of Lilienthal in the newspapers and noting the other significant aeronautical events of that year.

Lilienthal's death, and that of Englishman Percy Pilcher in October 1899, highlighted in the minds of the brothers that control was the key to safely mastering flight.

They devised a method of warping the wings to control roll; the warped wing produced more lift, causing a rolling motion to turn the aircraft in flight. A biplane kite, with a forward mounted elevator for pitch control, was built to test their ideas, which Chanute suggested they test on the mid-Atlantic coast to take advantage of the constant breezes, while the sand would cushion the impact of landing. The Wrights selected Kitty Hawk in North Carolina to conduct their tests, flying the glider initially as a tethered kite with either Wilbur or ballast carried aloft from early October 1900. Wilbur completed around a dozen free flights in the glider on October 20.

They returned to Kitty Hawk with a second glider in the summer of 1901. The aircraft had greater wing area and was flown in July and August, during which it demonstrated far less lift than predicated and tended to turn in the opposite direction to that desired. Back in Dayton the brothers conducted experiments to discover why lift was deficient, finding that the figure widely used for coefficient of air pressure (the Smeaton coefficient) was inaccurate. They investigated more efficient wing profiles, finding that longer, narrower surfaces offered better lift-to-drag ratios.

Armed with the new data, the 1902 glider was designed with a flatter airfoil of greater span and shorter chord. Initially a fixed rear rudder was added, but after adverse flight tests this was made movable and linked to the wing warping controls, enabling the pilot to aim the aircraft in the direction desired while banking and levelling out. The 1902 glider was tested at Kitty Hawk between September 20 until late October, demonstrating controlled turns following the modification of the rudder. The Wrights now had control of their machine in all three axes. On March 23, 1903, they applied for a patent for a "flying machine."

The Start of a New Era

The next phase was to add thrust. After failing to identify a sufficiently powerful and light engine, the Wright's shop mechanic Charlie Taylor built a powerplant in six weeks for their 1903 machine, which became known as the Wright Flyer. Weighing 180lb (82kg), it was capable of producing 12hp (9kW) and turned two hand-built propellers via drive chains.

The Wright Flyer was transported to Kill Devil Hills, 4 miles (6km) south of Kitty Hawk, in late 1903. During a ground test on November 5, the propeller shafts were damaged, and it was over a month before they were repaired and reinstalled on the aircraft.

On December 14, the Flyer was mounted on its dolly and, with Wilbur at the controls, was launched down the track laid on Big Kill Devil Hill. The aircraft was airborne for less than 4 seconds before stalling, coming down 105ft (32m) from its start point and sustaining slight damage. Repairs took three days.

It was Orville's turn next. The launching track was aligned into the wind on level ground early on December 17. At 1035hrs the Flyer was released to trundle down the track, lifting off after around 40ft (12m) at around 26mph (32km/h) into the 20mph (42km/h) wind. Orville was airborne for 12 seconds and covered 120ft (37ft). Only five people were on hand to witness the flight.

Two additional flights followed, of 12 and 15 seconds, increasing the distance covered to 175ft and 200ft (53m and 61m). Wilbur piloted the Wright Flyer for its fourth and last flight of the day, remaining airborne for 59 seconds and coming down 852ft (260m) from where he started. The front elevator supports broke on landing, while later the same day the Flyer was damaged beyond easy repair after repeatedly being blown over by a gust of wind. It would never fly again. But it had served its purpose; the age of powered heavier-than-air flight had begun.

CHAPTER 1

THE PIONEERS

INTRODUCTION

Controlled, powered, heavier-than-air flight was first achieved in the United States. On December 17, 1903, a machine built by two brothers from Ohio, Wilbur and Orville Wright, flew for 12 seconds over the sand dunes at Kill Devil Hills, North Carolina.

The Wrights continued to develop their design and conduct flights until November 1905, when they stopped in order to secure a patent and find customers for their machine. They did not fly again until 1908.

The brothers were not the only Americans seeking to create a flying machine, however. Across the states, individuals and groups worked on their own designs, most of which failed to make it into the air. Others were more successful, most notably Glenn Curtiss, a motorcycle racer and engine builder. By 1909, his pusher biplane design was among the most successful aircraft of the time. It sparked a patent infringement dispute with the Wrights that continued for years.

Witnessing exhibition flights or reading about them in the papers prompted others to attempt to build their own machines, or order one to be built for them. In June 1909, Curtiss sold the first aircraft in the United States and, two months later, the Wrights signed a deal with the US Army for the world's first military aircraft. These sales marked the start of the American aircraft industry.

WRIGHT FLYER

John T. Daniels' photograph of the first manned flight has become one of the most famous images ever taken, capturing the Wright Flyer in the air while Wilbur Wright looks on. Daniels, a member of the nearby lifesaving station, was one of a handful of observers at Kill Devil Hills in Dare County, North Carolina, at 1035hrs on December 17, 1903, when Orville Wright piloted the Wright Flyer. After traveling around 40ft (12m) along the 60ft (18m) rail track built for its launch, the Flyer rose at a ground speed of approximately 6mph (10km/h), dipped then climbed, before landing on the sand. In total, the first powered, controlled flight lasted just 12 seconds and the aircraft covered 120ft (37m). Three additional flights were made the same day, at the end of which Wilbur had extended the distance flown to 852ft (260m) during 59 seconds in the air, before landing hard and breaking the elevator support. While the aircraft was being manhandled back to camp, a gust of wind flipped the Flyer upside down, damaging it further.

AEA (CURTISS) AERODROME #3A *LOON*

The Aerial Experimental Association (AEA) was established on September 30, 1907, financed by Mabel Bell, wife of the inventor Alexander Graham Bell. Built by the AEA, Aerodrome #3 was designed by Glenn H. Curtiss to win the US$2,500 Scientific American Cup offered to the first person to complete a public flight of 1km (0.62 mile). The aircraft was named *June Bug* and Curtiss flew it to claim the prize on July 4, 1908. Both Alexander Bell and Curtiss wanted to create an aircraft that could operate from water, and added twin pontoons to *June Bug* between October and November 1908. Known as the Aerodrome #3A *Loon*, it was the first hydroplane. On November 28, an attempt was made to fly from Keuka Lake near Hammondsport in New York, but the aircraft could not reach sufficient speed to take off due to hydrodynamic drag. Further attempts were tried, but on January 2, 1909, water filled one of the pontoons and *Loon* sank. Although the aircraft was recovered, it was put into a boathouse for storage, where it rotted away.

CURTISS-HERRING NO. 1

Glenn Curtiss was approached by the Aeronautical Society of New York to create an aircraft for the 1909 Gordon Bennett Cup Race to be held at Reims in France during August. He assembled a larger variant of No. 1 *Golden Flyer* with a 63hp (47kW) Curtiss OX V-8 engine and lighter structure as the Curtiss-Herring No. 1. The aircraft, christened *Reims Racer*, was kept secret until the race, which involved flying against the clock over two circuits of the 10km (6.2 mile) closed course. Curtiss flew at a record speed of 43.35mph (69.76km/h), using the maneuverability of his aircraft to turn tightly at the corners and win the competition. Curtiss and *Reims Racer* went on to an air event at Brescia, Italy, in September 1909, winning several prizes, before the aircraft was shipped back to the United States. During October 1909, it was flown at the Los Angles International Air Meet at Dominguez Hills in California, the first in the country, during which a speed of 55mph (88km/h) was recorded. Curtiss sold the aircraft to Charles Keeney Hamilton, "the crazy man of the air," who was often drunk when flying. In *Reims Racer*, he became the first to fly an aircraft in Washington state on March 11, 1910, but he crashed into a lake in Seattle the next day while under the influence. Hamilton survived, but his aircraft did not.

CURTISS MODEL E

Glenn Curtiss (wearing the hat) at the controls of the US Navy's first aircraft, a Curtiss Model E, on Kekua Lake in Hammondsport, New York. Sitting at his side is Lieutenant Theodore Gordon Ellyson, "Naval Aviator No. 1," who was taught to fly at the Curtiss Flying School and became the first US naval pilot on June 30, 1911. The US Navy acquired 14 Model Es (as the Navy Type I) as its initial aircraft, the first gaining the serial number "A-1." After Curtiss completed the initial test hop in A-1 on July 1, Ellyson was taken aloft for a familiarization flight the same day, before completing two solo sorties. The A-1 had a single main float and two pontoons on the wing tips, although retractable wheels were later added. A-1 was used to establish a seaplane altitude record of 900ft (274m) on June 21, 1911, and was involved in many pioneering experiments, including being launched from an inclined wire on September 7, and trials with an early compressed-air catapult at Annapolis in Maryland, although the first test on July 31, 1912, ended with the aircraft and Ellyson in the Severn River. The aircraft completed 285 flights before it was damaged beyond repair in a crash on October 6, 1912.

LONGREN TOPEKA I

Inspired after witnessing a flight exhibition in June 1910, Albin Kasper Longren, along with his brother Ereanius and mechanic William Janicke, rented a room on the second floor of a building in Topeka, Kansas, in July 1911 to build a biplane powered by an eight-cylinder 60hp (45kW) Hall-Scott engine. Built in secrecy, the biplane was completed within five weeks and later designated Topeka I. The aircraft was dismantled and transported to a hayfield southeast of the city, where, on September 2, it was flown by Longren for 200ft (61m) at a height of 2ft (0.6m), the first successful flight in Kansas. Further flights were undertaken and, on September 8, the aircraft reached 200ft (61m) and flew for 6 miles (10km). Longren exhibited the Topeka I on barnstorming tours – for which he became known as the "Birdman of the Midwest" – to raise money to establish a firm to build aircraft. The first product of the Longren Aircraft Company was the Model AK, which appeared in 1921, but the company closed five years later.

MARTIN 1912 SEAPLANE

Glenn Luther Martin completed the first water-to-water flight on May 10, 1912. He flew a modified version of his Model 12, powered by a 15hp (11kW) Model V Ford engine, fitted with a pontoon instead of wheel landing gear, from Balboa Bay in Newport Bay, California, to Avalon Harbor on Catalina Island, a distance of 34 miles (55km) over the sea. Prior to departing, he took the precaution of handing his gold watch to the engineer Charlie Day, while his mother slipped an inflated bicycle tube over his shoulders "just in case." The initial leg was completed in 37 minutes, but the aircraft was damaged as it was dragged ashore, putting a hole in its pontoon. The patch used to cover the hole tore open on his return flight and, on landing back as close to the shore at Newport Bay as possible, the pontoon quickly filled with water, resulting in the aircraft settling up to its wings in the water. The flights set records for the longest hydroplane flight and longest over water round-trip, securing Martin US$100 for the feat. The aircraft is seen some time after the record-breaking flight, with Martin at the controls and a passenger behind. Martin founded the Glenn L. Martin Company in August 1912.

CURTISS MODEL F

The Curtiss Model F was one of the most numerous of the early flying boats, with more than 150 built to several different standards, followed by over 100 of the improved MF. The aircraft appeared in 1912, but the designation Model F only came into use the following year. This early example belonged to Gustave Maurice Heckscher, who entered it in the 1913 Great Lakes Reliability Cruise. The cruise lasted a week from July 8, with the entrants following the shoreline from Chicago to Detroit via the Straits of Mackinac. The aircraft featured a Goodier strut between the engine and forward hull structure to protect the crew from the powerplant in the event of a crash. The Curtiss F became the US Navy's standard flying boat trainer from April 1917, although it acquired its initial examples in 1913 as Navy Type Cs. They recorded many "firsts" with the service, including the first flight under automatic control on August 30, 1913, using a Sperry gyroscopic automatic pilot at Hammondsport, New York, and the first catapult launch from a warship under way, from USS *North Carolina* on November 5, 1915. The Curtiss F was also the first US military heavier-than-air aircraft used operationally, performing a scouting mission on April 25, 1914, during the Occupation of Veracruz in Mexico.

LOUGHEAD MODEL G

Allan and Malcolm Loughead rented a small garage at Pacific Ave and Polk Street on the waterfront of San Francisco to build their first aircraft, forming the Alco Hydro-Aeroplane Company with partners. The Loughead Model G was a tractor biplane completed as a floatplane with a six-cylinder Kirkham engine in 1913, with room for one (later two) passenger(s) as well as the pilot. The crankcase of the Kirkham engine split during ground runs and was replaced by an 80hp (60kW) Curtiss O V-8, enabling Allan to complete the Model G's first flight from San Francisco Bay on June 15, 1913. Later the same day, he took his brother aloft, followed by R. L. Coleman. The aircraft suffered minor damage in the summer of 1913, but was repaired and the original radiator replaced, before being put into storage for 18 months. The brothers, with the financial help of Mr. Meyer, purchased the aircraft outright from the other investors in the Alco Hydro-Aeroplane Company in early 1915 to fly passengers in the Panama-Pacific Exposition held in San Francisco, carrying 600 aloft on joyrides. The profit generated was used to create the Loughead Aircraft Manufacturing Company at Santa Barbara, California, from where the Model G continued to be used for joy flights. By 1918, the aircraft had deteriorated and was dismantled, with the Curtiss engine sold on.

BOEING B&W

William E. Boeing and US Navy engineer George Conrad Westervelt, assisted by Herb Munter, designed the B&W two-seat single-engine floatplane (named after the first letters of their surnames) from late 1915. Two were assembled at a boathouse on Lake Union in Seattle, Washington, built to house a Martin TA seaplane bought by Boeing, which was similar in external appearance to the B&W. The first B&W (seen here) was named *Bluebill* and made its first flight on June 29, 1916. The second aircraft, known as *Mallard*, made its maiden flight in November 1916. Although offered to the US Navy, the service declined to purchase the aircraft and both were sold to the New Zealand government in 1918 for the New Zealand Flying School, which operated them from Auckland's Waitemata Harbour. One of the aircraft also made the first official airmail flight in New Zealand on December 16, 1919. Westervelt was transferred by the US Navy to the east coast before the first B&W flew. With their partnership at an end, Boeing incorporated the Pacific Aero Products Company on July 15, 1916. On April 26, 1917, it was renamed the Boeing Airplane Company.

CESSNA *SILVER WINGS*

Clyde Vernon Cessna was an auto-dealer and mechanic in Enid, Oklahoma. In early 1911, he witnessed a flight demonstration in Oklahoma City and spoke to the aviator Roland Garros, who informed him that a copy of the Bleriot XI he was flying could be purchased from the Queen Aeroplane Company of New York, known as the Silver Queen. Cessna traveled to New York and worked at the company before acquiring a Silver Queen, which he shipped back to Enid, where an Elbridge Aero-Special four-cylinder engine was installed. The aircraft was named *Silver Wings* and, with an alarming number of crashes and repairs to the aircraft, Cessna taught himself to fly at Jet, Oklahoma, from May 1911. His persistence was rewarded with a flight of several miles on December 17, and he later appeared at a number of exhibitions. The repeated crashes and repairs meant that *Silver Wings* differed significantly from the stock Silver Queen and gave Cessna the confidence to build himself a new aircraft by 1913. In August 1916, he was offered an old railway car factory in Wichita, Kansas, owned by J. J. Jones Motor Company, in which to establish an aircraft factory and flying school.

CESSNA COMET

During 1916, Clyde Vernon Cessna was offered premises for his aviation operations in Wichita, Kansas, by John James Jones of the J. J. Jones Motor Car Company. In addition to premises to assemble his aircraft, Cessna was provided with an adjacent area of land from which to fly. During 1917, he worked on a two-seat aircraft with a partially enclosed cockpit for a passenger at the front of the 25ft (7.62m) long fuselage. Power was provided by a 60hp (45kW) Anzani engine. He flew his new aircraft on June 24 and, noting its high speed, named it "The Comet." Acknowledging the support provided by the automobile company, "Jones Six" was painted on the lower surfaces of the cotton fabric-covered wings in large letters to advertise the Jones Light Six automobile at the exhibitions it attended. Cessna is understood to have demonstrated the aircraft at around 30 such events. On July 5, 1917, while flying from Blackwell in Oklahoma back to Wichita, The Comet set an American national airspeed record of 124.62mph (200.5km/h). The flight also established a national record for distance of 76 miles (122km). By then, however, the United States had entered the war and the threat of fuel rationing meant that recreational flying would be strictly curtailed during the hostilities. As his aviation business appeared to have little future, Cessna returned to his family's wheat farm at Rago, Kansas, in late 1917. Had Walter Herschel Beech not tried to sell him a Laird Swallow five years later, the history of American general aviation could have been very different... Cessna and Beech hit it off and, along with Lloyd Stearman and a handful of investors, went on to form Travel Air in February 1925.

CHAPTER 2

THE AIRPLANE GOES TO WAR

INTRODUCTION

The second decade of the 20th century saw American aviation progress from its pioneering phase to the aircraft becoming a weapon of war.

The first Wright Flying School was opened on February 1, 1910, at Montgomery, Alabama, while the Burgess and Curtiss Co. of Marblehead, Massachusetts, became the first licensed aircraft manufacturer in the United States in February 1911, after authorization from the Wright Co. The Army received its first appropriation for aeronautics from Congress at the end of the following month, using the money to purchase five new aircraft. On May 8, 1911, the US Navy ordered its first aircraft from Glenn Curtiss. The Aviation Section of the Army Signal Corps was created on July 18, 1914.

While orders from the military services helped the nascent industry grow, the commercial potential of the aircraft was also being explored. A regular service between St. Petersburg and Tampa in Florida, using a Benoist flying boat, began on the first day of 1914. Although it was destined to operate for only three months, it was the first regular airline service in the country.

When the United States entered World War One on April 6, 1917, the Army lacked sufficiently modern combat aircraft. In May 1917, the War Department sent the Bolling Commission, headed by Raynal C. Bolling of United States Steel, to Europe to find an aircraft American industry could build. The Commission selected the Airco DH.4 – partly because a free license was granted by the British government. Throughout the war, the Air Service relied on foreign designs, with American industry primarily building trainers for the growing numbers of pilots needed. During the war, US industry built 11,750 aircraft.

CURTISS JN-4A "JENNY"

Probably the most famous aircraft produced by the American aircraft industry during World War One was the family of Curtiss "Jenny" trainers – its nickname coming from its JN designation. In addition to becoming the primary training aircraft for American pilots during the war, it went on to play a large role in the "barnstorming movement" of the early 1920s after surplus Jennies were acquired by owner-fliers. Curtiss created the JN by combining the best features of the earlier models J and N, with the new design entering service with the US Signal Corps in mid-1915. The most numerous basic model was the JN-4, which appeared in July 1916 and was built in several different versions for both domestic and foreign operators. The British Royal Naval Air Service (RNAS) and Royal Flying Corps (RFC) received several different versions. The first JN-4 variant was the JN-4B, which was followed by the JN-4A, 791 of which were built. The JN-4A was developed on behalf of the British and featured larger tail surfaces, revised fuselage, increased dihedral on the upper wings and ailerons on both sets, plus 6° of downthrust for the Curtiss OX-5 engine. JN-4A B1934 was one of a batch of around 160 JN-3/4/4As transferred from the RNAS to the RFC.

CURTISS HS-2L

The Curtiss HS series was one of the relatively small number of American-designed aircraft to be used operationally in Europe during World War One, flying anti-submarine patrols from France from June 1918. They also served from bases on the US Atlantic seaboard during the conflict, with a pair of HS-1Ls operating from Chatham in Massachusetts, making the only attack on a German U-boat in American waters during the war on July 21, 1918. The submarine escaped, however, as the weapons dropped by the flying boats failed to explode. The single-engine flying boat was built between 1917 and 1919 as a derivative of the unsuccessful twin-engined Curtiss H-14, the original Curtiss V-X-X engine in the HS-1 prototype being replaced by the Liberty in the HS-1L. The HS-2L introduced a longer wingspan that permitted a greater weight of bombs to be carried, its primary weapon against submarines. Just over half of the HS-1/2Ls produced were built by Curtiss, with others subcontracted to at least five firms, while postwar, the US Navy assembled some from its stockpile of spare parts. Around 1,175 were produced in total. This example, on the beach at Santa Barbara in California, was one of two assembled by the Loughead Aircraft Manufacturing Company before the end of the war. The company made a loss on its US$90,000 contract to build the flying boats, as it tried to improve upon the basic design, including experimenting with making the aircraft's fuel tanks bulletproof. HS-2Ls remained in service with the US Navy into 1928.

CURTISS H-12A "LARGE AMERICA"

The Curtiss H family was a series of flying boats with similar configurations, originally designed with the aim of claiming the £10,000 offered in 1913 by the British *Daily Mail* newspaper for the first nonstop crossing of the Atlantic by an aircraft. American businessman Rodman Wanamaker commissioned the Curtiss Aeroplane and Motor Company to produce the aircraft that would claim the prize. Glenn Curtiss collaborated with John Cyril Porte to scale-up the Model F, resulting in two Model Hs, the first of which, named *America*, was launched on June 22, 1914. Plans for the Atlantic flight had to be abandoned when war broke out in Europe, with Porte rejoining the British Royal Navy. There he persuaded the Admiralty to adopt the design as a long-range patrol aircraft. During the war, the basic configuration was developed in parallel in both America, by Curtiss, and the United Kingdom by Porte, initially for the RNAS. The American designs included the H-4 and the H-12 "Large America," the earlier aircraft retrospectively becoming known as "Small Americas." The H-12 appeared in late 1916 and was initially powered by a pair of 160hp (119kW) Curtiss V-X-X engines. It was considered underpowered by the British, who replaced the American engines with Rolls-Royce Eagle Is of 275hp (205kW) as the H-12A, and later the 375hp (280kW) Eagle VIII as H-12Bs. Curtiss H-12A 8681 was one of around 60 delivered to the RNAS, operating from Calshot in Hampshire in 1918.

CAPRONI CA 5

The American program to produce the Italian Caproni heavy bomber was extremely complex and ultimately failed. Although large production orders were placed with Curtiss and Fisher, they were eventually canceled and only five prototypes were assembled in the United States. Four prototype Ca 5s were ordered from Standard Aircraft Corporation of Elizabeth, New Jersey, in May 1918 as Standard Model E-3s, but only one was completed by the company and delivered in October 1918. A second was around 85 percent complete before being transferred to the Fisher Body Corporation of Detroit, Michigan, while the other pair were canceled. Fisher also received an order for three additional prototypes in August 1918. Caproni 40071 was the third of the three built by Fisher and was completed by early May 1919 without armament or bombing equipment. It was accepted on June 3 at Morrow Field in Detroit, and departed to McCook Field in Dayton, Ohio, three days later, where it was intended to be used by the Airplane Engineering Division. The Division never operated the aircraft, however, as it was quickly ordered to go to Ellington Field in Texas, where it arrived on June 20. There it was fitted with additional fuel tanks to increase range to around 750 miles (1,207km), but little use was made of the aircraft, and it is understood to have been out of service by late 1920.

CONTINENTAL KB-1

The KB-1 was developed by Vincent Justus Burnelli – born Buranelli, famous for his lifting body designs – and built by the Continental Aircraft Corporation of Long Island, New York, in 1916, of which Burnelli was the chief engineer and superintendent. The aircraft was built as a prototype to fulfill a US Army requirement for a reconnaissance aircraft. A tandem seat pusher biplane with open cockpits, with a tail supported by two steel booms, the aircraft had an unusual four-wheel landing gear. Power was provided by a single Hall-Scott A-5A of 135hp (101kW), propelling the KB-1 along at a maximum speed of 95mph (153km/h). Although Bertrand Blanchard Acosta, the chief instructor of the Aviation Section, US Signal Corps at Hazelhurst Field in Long Island, completed several successful flights of the KB-1 in freezing conditions above New York, the design was not selected for production by the US Army.

DAYTON-WRIGHT DH-4

The Airco DH.4 designed by Geoffrey de Havilland was selected as the standard US day bomber in 1917. A single example delivered to McCook Field in Dayton, Ohio, in August 1917 was fitted with a Liberty 12A, flying with that engine on October 29. It served as the prototype for the domestically produced variant, known as the DH-4. A total of 4,587 were built by the end of 1918 – more than three times the number of DH.4s assembled in Britain – of which 1,885 were shipped to France. The Dayton-Wright Airplane Co. of Dayton produced more than 3,100, with a further 1,600 by the Fisher Body Corporation and others by Atlantic Aircraft, Boeing, and Standard Aircraft. Postwar modifications resulted in more than 60 different variants of the DH-4, with 1,540 becoming DH-4Bs after the pilot's cockpit was repositioned. In the early 1920s, more than 300 were refurbished with steel tube fuselages as DH-4M versions. This aircraft appears to be a standard DH-4 belonging to the 3rd Aero Squadron, which arrived in the Philippines in August 1919 and operated from Camp Stotsenburg on Luzon. The unit was assigned to the 1st Group (Observation) in March 1920 and, the following year, was redesignated the 3rd Squadron (Pursuit) to provide coastal aerial defense.

CHRISTMAS BULLET

The Christmas Bullet was designed by Dr. William Whitney Christmas, who formed the Christmas Aeroplane Company in Washington, DC in 1910. Christmas claimed to have built two aircraft of his own design (though no evidence has been found of this). The company became the Durham Christmas Aeroplane Sales & Exhibition Company around 1912 and, in 1918, after moving to New York, the Cantilever Aero Company. After visiting the Continental Aircraft Company, Christmas proposed two designs, a single-seat scout and a three-crew "fighting machine." The scout became known (from February 1919) as the Christmas Bullet, a biplane with unbraced wings and sprung steel spars of all-wooden construction with a veneer-clad fuselage. The US Army was persuaded to loan the prototype Liberty 6 engine to power the aircraft, with the condition it would only be used for ground tests, a provision Christmas ignored. On its first flight in January 1919, the aircraft crashed when the wings folded, killing test pilot Cuthbert Mills and destroying the Liberty 6. A second prototype (seen here) powered by a Hall-Scott L-6 engine was built and displayed at the Aeronautical Exhibition at Madison Square Garden, New York, between March 1 and March 15, 1919, prior to its first flight. Lieutenant Allington Joyce Jolly was killed on its first flight in the Long Island area on April 27 after flying into a barn.

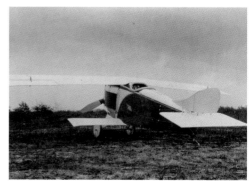

CHAPTER 3

THE ROARING TWENTIES

INTRODUCTION

The 1920s has been described as a time of "wealth and excess." It was a period when aviation was seen as glamorous, at the cutting edge of technology – when records were set and frequently broken – and the leading pilots of the day were household names.

World War One greatly increased the size of the American aircraft industry and the number of pilots in the country. Many who trained to fly at the expense of the government wanted to continue to do so after returning to civilian life, and this was facilitated by the availability of large numbers of military aircraft surplus at the end of the conflict. While the glut of airframes initially suppressed demand for new designs, increasing the troubles of an industry already struggling after the cancellation of large government contracts, several American manufacturers began to prosper after offering designs tailored to the needs of the private flier. By the middle of the decade, many new companies had been established to cash in on the boom.

Aircraft also became a practical method of transport during the decade, as commercial services developed – initially carrying the mail – with manufacturers responding by designing more efficient types able to carry greater loads and generate larger profits.

At the start of 1929, the future for the industry looked bright. This changed from that September, however, when prices on the New York Stock Exchange began to decline sharply. By the end of October, as the finances of many companies began to suffer, it was clear that difficult times lay ahead.

AEROMARINE 75 AERIAL CRUISER

Around eight Aeromarine 75 Aerial Cruisers were produced from 1920 by converting former US Navy Felixstowe F5L flying boats as airliners, powered by two 420hp (313kW) Liberty 12A engines, by the Aeromarine Plane and Motor Company. The company was formed in 1914 out of an aeronautical firm established by Inglis M. Upperçu at Keyport, New Jersey, in 1909. The Aerial Cruisers had a cabin for 11 passengers – although 27 were carried on one flight – with a crew of three. They had a range of around 340 miles (547km) and were operated by Aeromarine Airways. The airline was originally created in October 1920 as Aeromarine West Indies Airways from a merger of the manufacturer's subsidiary Aeromarine Sightseeing and Navigation Company and Florida West Indies Airways. It was renamed Aeromarine Airways in the spring of 1921. Operations by the airline started on November 1, 1920, flying from Key West in Florida to Havana in Cuba, the first scheduled international passenger and air mail service in the United States. The Cruisers also carried the first US Post Office international air mail from New York to Atlantic City, and from Cleveland to Detroit. Services to the Caribbean proved popular with passengers seeking to escape from the restrictions of prohibition. In early 1924, the mail contract was withdrawn, and Aeromarine Airways ceased operations soon after. The Aeromarine Plane and Motor Company became the Aeromarine-Klemm Corporation in 1928 in order to build the German Klemm light aircraft, but it ceased operations two years later.

LAWSON AIRLINER

Alfred William Lawson, previously a Major League baseball pitcher, formed the Lawson Airplane Company in South Milwaukee in Wisconsin, in April 1919. He is remembered for terming the phrase "air liner," producing the first such aircraft built in the United States and, in later life, some extremely outlandish ideas on the nature of reality. At a time when aircraft typically carried four people, Lawson planned to carry up to 16 passengers. The aircraft was assembled in the auto pavilion at the State Fair Park and was towed to the old Zimmerman farm, the site of Milwaukee's first municipal airfield. Powered by a pair of 400hp (298kW) Liberty L-12s, it flew to Ashburn field outside Chicago on August 27, 1919, its second flight, at the start of a publicity tour that involved flying many representatives of the media. It continued on to Toledo, Cleveland, Buffalo, and Syracuse, where it landed and came to rest nose down on September 4. The damage was slight and soon repaired and the aircraft flew on to Mitchell Field in New York on September 13, covering the 312 miles (502km) in 2 hours and 47 minutes, at 111mph (179km/h), then on to Bolling Field in Washington, DC. The Lawson airliner later made a forced landing at Collinsville in Pennsylvania on September 25, but was dismantled and shipped by rail to its target destination, Dayton in Ohio, for repair. The tour resumed on October 24, when it visited the Speedway racetrack in Indianapolis, then Chicago on November 6, with the airliner returning to Milwaukee eight days later. By then, Lawson was planning an even larger airliner, known as the Midnight Liner, for 24 passengers. Although built, it was destroyed taking off for its maiden flight on May 8, 1921. The Lawson Airplane Company ceased operations in 1922.

STOUT 2-AT PULLMAN

The Stout Engineering Company of Detroit, Michigan, created the first all-metal commercial aircraft in the United States, the 2-AT Pullman. Eleven were built, with the prototype named *Maiden Detroit* making its first flight on April 23, 1924, in the hands of Walter Edwin Lee at Selfridge Field, Michigan. During the flight, the windshield blew into the cockpit, jamming the controls and forcing Lee to force land on a frozen lake. After repairs, it was sold to the US Post Office, powered by a 500hp (373kW) Packard in place of the standard Liberty V-12 engine of 400hp (298kW). The Ford Air Transport Service purchased five Pullmans, all named *Maiden Dearborn* (the last four with suffixes I to IV) to fly between the company's factories. *Maiden Dearborn* completed the first scheduled service on April 13, 1925, carrying 1,000lb (454kg) of freight from Detroit to Chicago, and on July 31, Ford bought the company, which became the Stout Metal Airplane Division of the Ford Motor Co. *Maiden Dearborn* also flew the initial Contract Air Mail service, between Detroit and Cleveland on February 15, 1926, while the crash of *Maiden Dearborn I* in poor weather on May 18, 1926, had the dubious distinction of causing the first US commercial aviation fatality. Between September 28 and October 4, 1925, a Pullman was demonstrated at the First Annual Aerial Reliability Tour, partly sponsored by Ford, flying 1,900 miles (3,058km) between ten cities. This resulted in the sale of one to John Wanamaker & Co., which used it to carry passengers and freight between Philadelphia and New York. Four were also supplied to Florida Airways. In 1928, all Pullmans were grounded, after the US Department of Commerce declared that the wings were structurally unsafe.

HAMILTON METALPLANE H-45

Thomas Foster Hamilton established the Hamilton Aero Manufacturing Co. in Milwaukee, Wisconsin, in 1922, to produce propellers, floats, and various prototypes in Duralumin. The company name changed to Hamilton Metalplane Company in July 1927, but the company was taken over by the Boeing Airplane Co. in February 1929, although it continued to manufacture aircraft under its own name. The Hamilton Metalplane H-45 and slightly improved H-47 were fitted with a Pratt & Whitney Wasp and higher-powered R-1690 Hornet, respectively. They were designed by James S. McDonnell as all-metal transports, with corrugated Alclad skin, to carry six passengers and mail. The H-45 was certified in November 1928 and the H-47 the following month, and around 46 examples were produced. Northwest Airways was the first to put the H-45 into service, receiving an initial pair in September 1928, which it used on its route between St. Paul and Chicago. As additional aircraft were delivered, Northwest expanded its service into the Dakotas, Montana, and eventually Seattle, Washington. The carrier had eight H-45s in service by 1934; operators of the aircraft included Coastal Air Freight and Condor Air Lines, while Isthmian Airways based in the Panama Canal Zone used the aircraft on floats.

STINSON SM-1 DETROITER

In 1927, Paul Revere Braniff invested his life savings in Stinson SM-1 Detroiter NC1929, which was painted with Tulsa-Oklahoma City Airline titles. In partnership with his brother, Thomas Elmer, Paul founded the Oklahoma Aero Club, using the Stinson to transport its investors on hunting, fishing, and business trips, as well as to business meetings. While the Aero Club soon folded, on May 29, 1928, Paul R. Braniff Inc. was registered, with the intention of flying oil company executives between Oklahoma City Municipal Airport and Tulsa McIntyre Airport. The inaugural service was flown on June 20, 1928, with the airline flying two services there and back each day. A second Detroiter (NC7127) was purchased from Independence Air Transport by the summer of 1928. Detroiter NC1929 is seen towards the end of its career with Braniff, in the spring of 1929 at Tulsa McIntyre Airport (with the company's operation's manager, Paul Moore, in the cockpit and his son, Robert, behind). The aircraft was sold in May 1929, along with Paul R. Braniff Inc., to Universal Aviation Corporation of St. Louis, Missouri. It was last owned by Parks Air College and was canceled from the US register in July 1933. Braniff went on to become one of the United States's most famous airlines.

TRAVEL AIR 6000

The Travel Air Corporation of Wichita, Kansas, promoted the Travel Air 6000 as the "limousine of the air." Developed from the earlier 5000, the prototype Travel Air 6000 first flew on April 15, 1928. It was built in two main versions, both of which were also offered as floatplanes, with different engines. The Travel Air 6000A was powered by a Pratt & Whitney Wasp, while the 6000B used the Wright J-6-9, although most of the earlier aircraft were re-engined in service. While the Travel Air 6000 was initially aimed at executive and owner-operators, most of the approximately 150 built were supplied to regional airlines in the United States. Inter-City Air Lines of Springfield Airport in Massachusetts flew Travel Air 6000Bs between 1932 and 1933, including S-6000B NC385M (c/n 6B-2023). The aircraft was last registered to private owners in Newark, New Jersey, in July 1941. Travel Air was taken over by Curtiss-Wright in early 1930 when the Great Depression began to impact aviation sales. A further four airframes were built by Curtiss-Wright as Travel Air Sedan 6-Bs, plus another four by Airtech Flying Services of San Diego, California.

FAIRCHILD FC-2W2

Fairchild Aircraft Manufacturing of Farmingdale, New York, was established to build an aircraft suitable for aerial survey work. The prototype FC-1 flew in June 1926, but the original Curtiss OX-5 engine was replaced by a Wright J-4, with the aircraft becoming the FC-1A, which was put into production as the FC-2 with a larger cabin. Several different powerplants were offered, with the FC-2W using the Pratt & Whitney Wasp 410, replaced by the Wasp 420 in the FC-2W2, which also had greater cabin volume. The FC-2W2 was certified in August 1928 and – like other FC-2 derivatives – forged a reputation as a rugged aircraft able to operate in austere conditions. Fairchild FC-2W2 c/n 522 was registered to Canadian Colonial Airways of Montreal, Quebec, in Canada, as G-CAVN on September 29, 1928. The airline was founded on March 6, 1928, to operate Foreign Air Mail Route No.1 between New York and Montreal, starting on October 1, 1928. By early 1930, the aircraft had passed to Canadian Airways. While making a precautionary landing at Riverside-Albert, New Brunswick, on February 19, 1930, during bad weather and with a shorting battery, the aircraft caught fire and was damaged beyond repair. All the occupants managed to escape unhurt.

CHAPTER 5
CIVIL AVIATION COMES OF AGE

INTRODUCTION

Commercial aviation grew out of its infancy in the 1930s. It was a period of rapid technological advances; the biplane gave way to the monoplane, fixed landing gears were replaced by retractable units, and the power and reliability of engines greatly improved.

The growth of the airlines, with their demands to carry more faster, further – and safer – helped spur the development of aviation. By the start of the 1930s, the airlines had largely succeeded in demonstrating that air transport was viable and attractive to the public. They had yet to work out exactly how to make it economically viable, however, with many carriers relying on contracts to carry the mail to turn a profit. What they needed was more efficient aircraft.

At the start of the decade, a typical airliner, the Boeing 80A trimotor biplane, could cruise at 125mph (201km/h), fly 460 miles (740km) and carry up to 12 passengers. The breakthrough came with the Boeing 247 and the competing Douglas DC-2, which appeared in 1933 and 1934, respectively, and combined the requirements of comfort, safety, and speed, but, more importantly, increased operating profits. The appearance of the Douglas DC-3 in late 1935 – able to carry 50 percent more passengers than the DC-2 – finally gave the airlines what they had long desired, and, by the end of the decade, even better airliners were becoming available. On the last day of 1938, the four-engined Boeing 307 monoplane completed its first flight. It had a cruise speed of 222mph (357km/h) and a range with a maximum payload of 1,675 miles (2,695km). Up to 33 passengers could be carried in a fully pressurized cabin.

FORD 5-AT-C TRIMOTOR

Henry Ford bought the Stout Metal Airplane Company and its designs in 1925. Work to turn the single-engine Stout 2-AT Pullman into a trimotor as the Stout 3-AT was not successful, although it was notable as the first all-metal trimotor built in America. The prototype was destroyed on January 16, 1926, when the Stout factory burned down, and the aircraft was redesigned as the much more successful 4-AT. Ford went on to assemble 199 Trimotors of many different subtypes. Ford 5-AT-C c/n 5-AT-68 was built at Dearborn in Michigan by the Stout Metal Airplane Division of the Ford Motor Company, making its first flight on August 3, 1929. It was used as a demonstrator as NC409H for a year before being registered as G-ABFF to the British sales agent, Harold S. Cooper, in October 1930, although this was changed to G-ABHF to incorporate Henry Ford's initials in January 1931. In October 1934, the Trimotor was sold to Guinea Airways, one of two acquired by the airline, arriving at Lae in New Guinea the following month, where it was reassembled with a modified cabin roof hatch that could be removed to enable bulky cargo to be loaded in place of the 14 passenger seats. It was reregistered as VH-UTB on December 10, 1934, flying its first service with Guinea that day between Lae and Port Moresby. The Trimotor continued to fly in New Guinea, except for a brief detachment to the airline's operation at Adelaide in South Australia in early to mid-1937. It was finally destroyed in a crash at Little Wau Creek in New Guinea on October 23, 1941.

LOCKHEED 5C VEGA

Lockheed Model 5B Vega NR105W was acquired by the oil driller Florence C. Hall on June 21, 1930. He named it *The Winnie Mae of Oklahoma* after his daughter. Hall hired Wiley Hardeman Post to fly the aircraft, who entered it in the National Air Races, setting a record of 9 hours, 9 minutes, and 4 seconds flying between Los Angeles and Chicago on August 27. Post was accompanied by navigator Harold Gatty for a 14-stop round-the-world record flight in the Vega. The pair set off from New York on June 23, 1931, and made stops in Canada, England, Germany, Russia, Siberia, Alaska, Canada, and Cleveland in Ohio, before landing back in New York on July 1. The flight was completed in 8 days, 15 hours, and 51 minutes. Hall was delighted – he presented the Vega to Post in appreciation. During 1932, the aircraft was upgraded as a Model 5C for operations at higher weights, while a radio compass and autopilot were installed to reduce the workload during long distance flights and was used by Post to complete a second round-the-world flight. Post departed New York on July 15, 1933, and by making only 11 stops, he was able to cut the time to 7 days, 18 hours, and 49 minutes. The aircraft was later used for long-distance, high-altitude flights, equipped with a supercharged engine and jettisonable landing gear, instead landing on a metal-covered spruce landing skid glued to the fuselage. During such flights, Post wore a pressure suit designed by the B. F. Goodrich Company, which saw the Vega propelled along at speed within the jetstream. *The Winnie Mae* was donated to the Smithsonian Institution in 1936 by Post's wife after he perished in a crash on August 15, 1935.

STEARMAN-NORTHROP 4A ALPHA

The Alpha was designed by John K. "Jack" Northrop as an all-metal passenger aircraft, with room for up to six in the cabin, although the pilot remained exposed to the elements. It was introduced into service as the Alpha 2 airliner and was later developed into the Alpha 3 mixed passenger/cargo aircraft. The Alpha 4 had a longer wingspan and streamlined undercarriage. Its relatively high speed and good reliability resulted in 17 Alphas of all models being built, but as larger, more capacious airlines became available, the type was relegated to carrying freight. This resulted in the all-cargo Alpha 4A, which was created by removing the cabin windows and increasing the gross weight of existing, earlier variants. Alpha NC11Y was the third built. It was rolled out in November 1930 and became the personal aircraft of Assistant Secretary of Commerce for Aeronautics Colonel Clarence Marshall Young. It later passed to the Ford Motor Company and National Air Transport, before being sold to TWA. TWA withdrew the Alpha in 1934, and NC11Y was sold to Frederick B. Lee, who hoped to fit it with floats and fly it around the world. Lee's plan did not come to fruition, however, and he sold the aircraft on, with it passing through several owners and falling out of use. In May 1946, it was purchased and stored by Foster Hannaword, Jr., of Winnetka, Illinois. When Hannaword passed away in 1971, it was gifted to the Experimental Aircraft Association in Hales Corners, Wisconsin, before being acquired by the Smithsonian. During 1975, the aircraft was restored by TWA and was placed on display at the National Air and Space Museum in Washington, DC.

LOCKHEED ALTAIR 8D

The Lockheed Altair introduced the modern retractable landing gear. Unlike on earlier aircraft fitted with the device, the gear closed into the wing flush with the undersides, rather than into the side of the fuselage or to the rear and partially protruding. Lockheed created the Altair after a Sirrus was ordered by Charles Lindbergh. He wanted a retractable undercarriage mounted in a redesigned wing instead of the standard fixed gear. While the wings were built, they were not fitted to his aircraft. Instead, the specially built unit was mated to a Lockheed-owned Sirius 8A (NR119W, c/n 153) powered by a Pratt & Whitney Wasp C to create the prototype Altair 8D (X119W). Flight testing by pilot Marshall Headle began in late September 1930, after ground testing of the gear with the aircraft mounted on jacks. For the next six months, it was evaluated by Lockheed, with Vance Breese setting an unofficial record between Oakland and Burbank of 92 minutes. The Wasp C was replaced by a B model engine before the aircraft was loaned to the US Army Air Corps. An attempt by Captain Ira C. Eaker to break the transcontinental speed record on April 11, 1931, was thwarted by problems with the supercharger. Re-engined again with a Pratt & Whitney R-1340-7, the Altair was sold to the Army in November 1931 as the YIC-25 (32-393). It was damaged beyond repair seven months later. Four more Sirius airframes were also modified with the new landing gear, while a further six Altairs were built as such.

VULTEE V-1A SPECIAL

Marshall Headle made the maiden flight of the prototype Vultee V-1 on February 19, 1933, and an additional 26 examples of the design were built. V-1A NC13770 was the eighth produced, one of 10 ordered by American Airlines. On January 14-15, 1935, the aircraft was used by James H. "Jimmy" Doolittle to set a Fédération Aéronautique Internationale world record for speed over a recognized course of 205.04mph (329.98km/h) while flying between the Union Air Terminal at Burbank, California, and Floyd Bennet Field in New York (although he landed at Newark Airport in New Jersey). The flight had a duration of 11 hours, 59 minutes, during which Doolittle was accompanied by his wife and Robert Adamson, an executive of the Shell Oil Company, which had leased the aircraft from American Airlines for the record attempt. By 1936, the aircraft had been sold to Harry Richman of Miami Beach in Florida, becoming NR13770 as a V-1A Special after a Pratt & Whitney Wasp was installed, and christened *Lady Peace*. It was one of seven acquired in 1937 by the Vimalert Company for supply to the Spanish Republican forces, four of which were loaded onto the motorship *Mar Cantábrico* in New York. The vessel was captured by the Nationalists enroute to Spain and the V-1As were put into service with 43º Grupo de Transporte y Enlace (43rd Liaison and Transport Group). *Lady Peace* became *Capitán Haya*, initially coded "18-7," and later "43-14." Spain continued to fly V-1As until 1941.

BOEING 247D

Much faster than the trimotors it replaced, the Boeing 247 was the first low-wing multi-engined American transport, with room for 10 passengers in the cabin. The first flew on February 8, 1933, after an order for 70 was placed the previous year by United Air Lines (UAL) for the various companies within its group. Of these, 59 were completed as Boeing 247s and the rest as 247Ds with NACA cowlings, controllable pitch propellers, revised cockpit canopies, and fabric (rather than metal) covered control surfaces. The Boeing 247 entered service on May 22. Lufthansa also received two 247s, while the sole 247A went to Pratt & Whitney as a test bed and executive transport. All except those for Germany were later upgraded as 247Ds (although some never received the new windshield). Boeing 247D NR257Y was ordered by UAL and first flew on September 5, 1934, but was completed with extra tanks in the cabin for entry into the 1934 MacRobertson air race from London to Melbourne, Victoria, Australia, by Colonel Roscoe Turner and Clyde Pangborn. The pair, plus Reeder Nichols, departed RAF Mildenhall in Suffolk in the aircraft on October 20. Their time of 92 hours, 55 minutes, and 30 seconds placed them third overall and second in the transport category. The aircraft was later returned to UAL, becoming NC13369, but was sold to the Union Electric Company of St. Louis, Missouri, in January 1936, before going to the Department of Commerce Air Safety Board as NC11 in August 1939. In July 1953, it was donated to the Smithsonian Institute and is currently on display at its National Air and Space Museum in Washington, DC.

DOUGLAS DC-2

The prototype Douglas Commercial 2 (DC-2) first flew on May 11, 1934, and just under 200 were produced, around one-third of which were delivered to US military services. The airliner was a development of the original DC-1, designed in response to TWA's requirement for an equivalent to the Boeing 247, but was longer and more powerful than the original aircraft and could carry 14 passengers. TWA became the launch customer with an order for 20, while American Airlines and several European carriers followed suit. American Airlines initially signed for ten DC-2-120s, which were delivered in November and December 1934, including NC14278. Between May and August 1935, a further eight were handed over. On May 10, 1941, the airliner was sold to the British Purchasing Commission. It was due to become G-AGCG with BOAC, but the civil registration was not applied. Instead, the British military marking HK867 was allocated for service with No. 267 Squadron in Egypt. It was officially transferred to Pan American Airways-Africa as "US3" on July 25, 1941, the airline being tasked with ferrying the aircraft to its new operator. Unfortunately, it never reached the Middle East, as on September 7, 1941, during the delivery flight, the DC-2 was hit by a Hawker Hurricane and written off at Hastings Site, outside Freetown in Sierra Leone.

LOCKHEED 10A ELECTRA

Hanford-Rapid Airlines of Sioux City put its fleet of Lockheed 10A Electras into service on July 10, 1936, configured to carry ten passengers. During 1938, the airline was renamed Mid-Continental Airlines, by which time the fleet was used on The Kansas Citian and The Dakotan services. *Chippewa Chief*, a Lockheed 10A Electra of Mid-Continental Airlines, is seen about to depart the airline's base at Sioux City, Iowa. Only 16 Electras remained in service with five airlines – including Mid-Continental – when the US entered World War Two. The aircraft being worked on in the background, Model 10A NC14260, was originally delivered to Northwest Airlines on December 21, 1934, before being sold to Mid-Continental in November 1937. It was impressed by the US Army Air Corps as a C-36A (later UC-36A) in June 1942 as 42-56638, going to National Airlines in 1944 with the same American civil registration. The following year, Springfield Feeder Lines acquired the aircraft, flying it until 1952. In 1953, it went to the Honduran Air Force as FAH-104, before returning to the United States in 1960 as N6106A, then becoming N4963C two years later. In 1972, it was acquired by the US Air Force Museum. It is currently displayed at the Pima Air and Space Museum at Tucson, Arizona.

DOUGLAS DOLPHIN

Wilmington-Catalina Airline was the first commercial operator of the Douglas Dolphin, purchasing two Model 1s. The aircraft first flew in September 1930 and was issued a type certificate on May 9, 1931. The amphibians were used to carry up to six passengers between Wilmington in Los Angeles (as seen here) and Avalon Bay on Catalina Island off the coast of California, a distance of only 20 miles (32km) covered in 12 minutes, at that point the shortest commercial schedule route in the United States. The cabins of the aircraft were later reconfigured to accommodate eight people as the Model 1 Specials. Two Dolphins were also delivered to the China National Aviation Corporation (a Pan American subsidiary), while others were built for wealthy owners as luxury transports, including William Edward Boeing (of the Boeing Company), radio broadcasting pioneer Powel Crosley, Jr., and Philip Knight "P. K." Wrigley (the son of the owner of the chewing gum company), while William Kissam and Alfred Gwynne Vanderbilt each acquired one and both were based on their yacht *Alva*. Somewhat ironically – given that it was an amphibian – the largest fleet went to the US Army Air Corps, which put successive variants into service as the YIC-21, YIC-26, YIC-26A, C-26B and C-29. The US Coast Guard operated 13 RD-1/-2/-4s, while the US Navy accepted an RD-1, three RD-2s and six RD-3s. One of the RD-2s was the first aircraft acquired for the use of an American president, although it is unconfirmed if Franklin D. Roosevelt was ever flown in it.

CONSOLIDATED MODEL 28-1

Two Model 28s wore the registration NC777, both named *Guba*, and produced for the zoologist and explorer Richard Archbold. The aircraft were acquired for Archbold's third expedition to Dutch New Guinea – "Guba" means "sudden storm" in the local Motu dialect. Permission from the US Navy to buy the first aircraft, a Model 28-1 similar to the PBY-1 but without military equipment, was granted on January 2, 1937. It was completed in June 1937, becoming the largest privately-owned aircraft in the world at that point, flying from Lake Mead in California on the 18th of the month. It completed the first nonstop transcontinental flight by a flying boat on June 24, between San Diego and Queens in New York, landing off North Beach after 17 hours and 3 minutes in the air. It was destined not to join Archbold's expedition, however. On August 13, 1937, Sigizmund Aleksandrovich Levanevsky and his crew of five, flying in the Bolkhovitinov DB-A, disappeared during a flight over the North Pole. The Soviet government asked Archbold to sell it the Model 28 to help search for the missing fliers, to which he agreed. From August 18, the Australian polar explorer Sir Hubert Wilkins operated the Model 28 from Coppermine in the Northwest Territories, Canada, flying 19,000 miles (30,578km) over a month during the search for the lost fliers. No trace of the DB-A or Levanevsky's crew was ever found. The Model 28-1 (as URSS L-2) was later flown back to New York, where it was dismantled and shipped to the Soviet Union in late 1937. Around the same time, a replacement *Guba* was delivered to Archbold.

BOEING 314A CLIPPER

Pan American Airways' (Pan Am) requirement for a transoceanic transport resulted in Boeing designing a large, four-engine flying boat from 1935, using the same basic wing design as the XB-15 bomber. The airline signed for six Boeing 314s on July 21, 1936, the first flying on June 7, 1938, originally with a single tail that was later replaced by endplate fins and a larger central unit. Transatlantic airmail services began on May 20, 1939, while the first passengers were carried on June 28, making the Boeing 314 the largest aircraft in regular airline service at the time. Although up to 70 passengers could be carried, plus a crew of ten, the overnight services usually accommodated 40 sleepers. A further six improved Boeing 314As were also delivered to Pan Am by January 20, 1942, and five 314s were later updated to the new standard. Three Boeing 314As were sold to British Overseas Airways Corporation (BOAC) in August 1940 prior to delivery and were handed over the following year, NC18608 becoming G-AGCA *Berwick*. In mid-1942, Prime Minister Winston Churchill and Minister of Aircraft Production Lord Beaverbrook flew in *Berwick* back from the United States following its entry into World War Two. After the war, BOAC continued to use the three aircraft between New York and Baltimore, Maryland, and onto Bermuda until January 1948. BOAC's three Boeing 314As were sold to the brokerage firm General Phoenix Corporation of Baltimore in April 1948, before going to World Airways. That charter airline folded the following year and NC18608 (along with six other Boeing 314As) was stored at San Diego in California, where it was scrapped in 1952.

VOUGHT-SIKORSKY VS-44

The Vought-Sikorsky VS-44A was the last of a long line of large Sikorsky flying boats. It was developed from the XPBS-1 patrol-bomber prototype by Michael Gluhareff. Work to build three commercial examples as VS-44As began in February 1940 for American Export Airlines, which wanted to fly them between New York and Lisbon in Portugal. A mock-up was displayed at the World's Fair in New York, which opened on April 30, 1939. The first VS-44A was named *Excalibur* on January 17, 1942, and it was taken aloft for its maiden flight the following day. Flight tests began in earnest in March 1942, with the first transatlantic test flight that June. When the United States entered the war, it was planned that all three would go to the US Navy as XJR2S-1s, but it was later decided that all three would be operated by American Export Airlines under contract to the service. *Excalibur* was lost during a take-off accident departing England in October 1942. The second, *Excambian*, survived the war but was abandoned at Lima, Peru, after it was sold to Tampico Airlines in 1949. It was later rescued for Avalon Air Transport (later Catalina Air Lines) and underwent a rebuild in 1957 as *Mother Goose* for service between Long Beach in Los Angeles and Avalon Bay on Catalina Island, carrying 47 passengers. In 1967, it was sold to Antilles Air Boats, which flew it until it was extensively damaged on January 3, 1969. VS-44A NC41882 was the last of the three built and was named *Exeter*. It too operated as transport throughout the war from La Guardia Field in New York. In 1946, it was sold to TACI (Transporte Aéreo de Carga Internacional) of Uruguay, becoming CX-AIR, but was destroyed on August 15 after crashing on the River Plate near Montevideo.

BUDD BB-1 PIONEER

The Edward G. Budd Manufacturing Company of Philadelphia, Pennsylvania, built railway vehicles, making use of large amounts of stainless steel. Keen to capitalize on its expertise with the material, Budd began to explore aeronautical applications for stainless steel using shot-welding techniques. A license was acquired to build the Italian Savoia-Marchetti S.56 light amphibian with the idea of replacing the wooden structure with stainless steel. The aircraft was constructed as the Budd BB-1 Pioneer (NR749N) during 1930, powered by a single five-cylinder Kinner C-5 of 210hp (160hp), becoming the first aircraft constructed from stainless steel. A wire-cloth fabric was initially applied over the steel frame wings, but it proved impossible to tighten and was quickly replaced by fabric. The aircraft made its first flight from a field northwest of Philadelphia, known as the Budd Aerodrome, in 1931 and was extensively tested by the company in the summer of 1932. It was found to be challenging to operate from water. After being exhibited across the United States, the aircraft was transported to Europe, flying over the Alps from France to Italy and back. In 1935, after logging 1,700 flight hours, the aircraft was donated to The Franklin Institute in Philadelphia, where it was mounted outside with its wings stripped of its outer fabric. It has remained there ever since, although it was removed from its poles for restoration in both 1969 and 2016, last going back on external display on December 1, 2017.

WACO KNF

Waco Aircraft Co. of Troy, Ohio, produced a number of attractive biplanes in the late 1920s and into the 1930s. The Waco Model F was designed to be built in several different versions, differing only forward of the firewall in the make of engine installed. The Waco KNF fitted with a 100hp (75kW) Kinner K5 was the cheapest option to operate, although it was only 10hp less powerful than the Warner Scarab-powered RNF developed in parallel. The other initial member of the F family was the INF, which had a more powerful Kinner B-5. The KNF was certified in the United States on December 4, 1930, and the wider Model F family went on to outsell every open-cockpit biplane in the United States in 1930–31. Easy to fly and responsive, the KNF found a market as a pilot trainer, where its ability to absorb a lot of punishment was much appreciated. Production of the KNF is understood to have totaled around 20 aircraft.

STINSON SR-7 RELIANT

Stinson created the SR-7 Reliant by mating the fuselage of the earlier SR-6 Reliant with a scaled version of the wing of its Model A trimotor, giving rise to its popular (but unofficial name) of "Gull Wing." Customers could choose between three different Lycoming engine powered models: the SR-7A with a 225hp (168kW) R-680-4 could carry four occupants, while the SR-7B and -7C, with a 245hp (183kW) R-680-6 or 260hp (194kW) R-680-5, respectively, could both carry five. The type certificate for the SR-7B was issued on February 13, 1936, and Stinson built more than 50 of the three models in total. SR-7B Reliant CF-AYW was delivered around mid-1936 to General Airways of Toronto, Canada, which was formed in 1928 by Captain Roy Brown, who was famously credited with shooting down Manfred von Richthofen, the Red Baron, during World War One. Stinson tested its floatplanes on Belleville Lake, located not far from its factory at Wayne in Michigan, and CF-AYW was flown from the body of water in April 1936. General Airways operated the Reliant until it force-landed on a road following an engine failure near Rouyn in Québec on September 9, 1937, after which it was sold to George A. Thorne, Jr., of Chicago, Illinois, as NC1383. Thorne had been a member of the 1929 Admiral Byrd Expedition to the Antarctic. He was killed when the Reliant crashed into a wood at Harrisville, New Hampshire, on September 7, 1939, with the subsequent fire also destroying several acres of woodland.

PIPER J-3 CUB

The Piper J-3 Cub was developed from the earlier J-2 by Walter Corey Jamouneau. It entered production at the company's new factory at Lock Haven in Pennsylvania, a fire having destroyed the previous premises on March 16, 1937. From early-1938, Piper offered three models of the J-3: the Cub Trainer, Cub Sport, and Cub Seaplane. The aircraft was offered with a range of engines from Continental (as the J-3C), Franklin (J-3F), Lycoming (J-3L), and Lenape (J-3P/R), starting with 40hp (30kW) models certified on October 31, 1937, and 50hp (37kW) powerplants from July 14, 1938. Continental later modified its engine slightly to produce 65hp (48.5kW), enabling Piper to offer the J-3C-65 in 1940. Civil production of the J-3C-65 ended in 1942 – during which nearly 300 were delivered to flying schools – and the line instead began turning out the military O-59 Grasshopper variant for the US Army Air Forces, which quickly redesignated the aircraft as L-4. Over 5,400 L-4s were delivered, plus 250 NE-1/2s for the US Navy, while a further 253 unpowered TG-8s were produced as training gliders. Cubs were also used to provide elementary flight training for pilots within the Civilian Pilot Training Program, which became the War Training Service when the United States entered the conflict and continued until the summer of 1944. By the end of World War Two, around 80 percent of all US pilots had learned to fly on the Cub. A total of 19,888 of all versions of the J-3 were eventually built by Piper, with the last J-3C-65 delivered by the company in 1947. The basic airframe formed the basis of many of Piper's subsequent models.

CESSNA C-145 AIRMASTER

For the 1939 season, Cessna introduced several changes to its previous C-38 model. These included improved wing panels, the deletion of the belly-flap in favor of split-type wing units, and hydraulic wheel brakes. Originally known as the C-39 (for 1939), the first was rolled out on September 11, 1938. The designation was soon changed to C-145 to reflect the horsepower of the Warner Super Scarab and the name Airmaster was adopted. The C-145 was certified in the United States on October 1, 1938. A variant powered by a 165hp (123kW) version of the Super Scarab was approved as the C-165 in March 1939. Production continued until late 1941–early 1942, during which time some 80 of both models were built, before the need to expand wartime production of the T-50 Bobcat brought an end to the line. Airmaster NC21912 (c/n 552) was built and delivered in 1940. In July 1948, a new certificate of airworthiness was issued for the aircraft, which was then registered to Stephen V. Miskoff. Its US civil registration was canceled in November 1955.

GRANVILLE GEE BEE R-1 SUPER SPORTSTER

Granville Brothers Aircraft of Springfield, Massachusetts, is best known for a series of racers, although it started in 1929 designing and building a biplane side-by-side trainer, the Model A. This was followed by a succession of "Sportsters" built in the early 1930s, which were successful in a number of races and events across the United States. The brothers – Zantford, Thomas, Robert, Mark, and Edward – created the Model Z Super Sportster to win the Thompson Trophy at the National Air Races at Cleveland, Ohio, in 1931. Lowell Bayles lifted the Trophy on September 7. Bayles was killed in the aircraft that December while attempting to capture the world speed record for landplanes; he did, but not by a large enough margin to be registered. The R-1 and R-2 Super Sportsters were built for the 1932 competition, with a wide, teardrop-shaped fuselage in an effort to reduce drag. The R-1 was flown by Jimmy Doolittle to victory at the 1932 Thompson Trophy race, while also claiming the speed record at 296mph (476km/h) during the Shell Speed Dash. On July 1, 1933, the R-1 stalled and crashed after departing Indianapolis during the transcontinental Bendix Trophy race, killing pilot Russell Boardman. The aircraft was rebuilt with an 18in (46cm) longer fuselage, which was mated to the original wings of the R-2 as the R-1/2 "Longtail." Soon after it was completed, it was damaged after over-running the runway while landing, pilot Roy Minor surviving the accident. With no money to repair the aircraft, it was sold to Cecil Allen, who added new wings and named it *Spirit of Right*. Allen was killed in the aircraft during the 1935 Burbank to Cleveland Bendix Trophy race.

HUGHES H-1 (1B) RACER

Howard Hughes employed Glenn Odekirk during the making of the epic war film *Hell's Angels* to look after the vast fleet of aircraft used in the production. From 1934, along with Richard Palmer, they designed a sleek monoplane for an attempt on the airspeed record, which became known as the Hughes H-1 or 1B. Constructed with flush rivets to produce a smooth finish and incorporating a retractable landing gear and landing skid, the aircraft was fitted with a specially tuned Pratt & Whitney R-1535 radial engine capable of providing over 1,000hp (749kW), over 30 percent more than its standard output. Its wings were interchangeable between short span units for speed and longer ones for cross-country flights. Hughes completed the first flight on September 13, 1935, at Martin Field in California, raising the landplane speed record to 352.39mph (567.12km/h). He ran out of fuel, however, coming down near Santa Ana without injury or significant damage to the aircraft. It was repaired and, on January 19, 1937, Hughes piloted it between Los Angeles in California and New York City in 7 hours, 28 minutes, and 25 seconds to set a transcontinental record at an average speed of 322mph (518km/h). The H-1 was then put into store at the Hughes facility at Culver City, California, where it remained until 1975, when it was donated to the Smithsonian Institute and placed on display at the National Air and Space Museum in Washington, DC.

PITCAIRN PCA-2

From 1929, Harold F. Pitcairn held manufacturing licenses from Juan de la Cierva for the autogiro, which he put into production at the Pitcairn-Cierva Autogiro Co. in Willow Grove, Pennsylvania. The two- to three-seat Pitcairn PCA-2, powered by a 330hp (250kW) Wright R-975-J6-9 Whirlwind, became the first autogiro to receive a type certificate in the United States on April 2, 1931. Around 20 were built, with the first sold going to the *Detroit News* newspaper. Many performed notable flights. John M. Miller completed the first flight across America by a rotorcraft in PCA-2 *Missing Link* on May 19, 1931. *Miss Champion* was PCA-2 number 27, delivered in June 1931 to the Champion Spark Plug Company and flown by Captain Lewis A. Yancey to promote the company's wares throughout the rest of the year. This included flying 6,500 miles (10,461km) between 38 cities in 28 states during the Ford National Reliability Air Tour. In January 1932, it was flown to Havana in Cuba, then on to Mexico, where it was used to hunt for sites of archaeological interest. Yancey also raised the altitude record for rotary-wing aircraft, to 21,500ft (6,553m), over Boston, Massachusetts, on September 25, 1932. He also operated the autogiro from a site in Yosemite Park, California, surrounded by 3,000ft (914m) cliffs, to demonstrate the autogiro's ability to operate from confined areas. It was retired in 1932, going to Chicago's Museum of Science and Industry, but was sold after World War Two to a private owner. In 1982, it was acquired by Steve Pitcairn, Harold's son, who restored it to flying condition. It was donated to the Experimental Aircraft Association (EAA) AirVenture Museum at Oshkosh, Wisconsin, in September 2005.

VOUGHT-SIKORSKY VS-300

Igor Sikorsky, his hat firmly attached to his head, was at the controls of the prototype Vought-Sikorsky VS-300 helicopter for its first flight on September 14, 1939, at Stratford, Connecticut. The helicopter was tethered to the ground "just in case," but the flight only lasted a few seconds, and Sikorsky managed to land without damage to either himself or the aircraft. The first free flight of the design occurred on May 13, 1940, making the VS-300 the first successful American helicopter. Many changes were incorporated in the design as flight testing progressed. Its bare frame was later covered by fabric, although the rear was left exposed. Amphibious floats were also added, the aircraft making the first take-off and landing from water on April 17, 1941. An airfoil section was attached to the tail to help counter the main rotor's torque, but this was found to be ineffective and was later removed. The VS-300 claimed the world endurance record for a rotary-wing aircraft on May 6, 1941, staying airborne for 1 hour, 32 minutes, and 26 seconds, beating that set in a Focke-Wulf Fw 61 in 1938. On October 7, 1943, the prototype VS-300 was presented to Henry Ford for inclusion in his Edison Museum at Dearborn in Michigan. The helicopter remains on display at the renamed Henry Ford Museum.

CHAPTER 6

COMBAT AIRCRAFT OF THE 1930s

INTRODUCTION

The 1930s was dominated by the Great Depression, a widespread and long-lasting economic downturn. For military aviation, it was a time of great technological advances, with the rate of improvement gathering pace as the decade progressed.

The US Army Air Corps had 1,700 aircraft and the US Navy and Marine Corps just over 1,200 in mid-1932. At the time, both services operated biplane combat aircraft exclusively, a situation that continued until the Boeing P-26 "Peashooter" entered service in late 1933. Not only was the pursuit ship a monoplane, it was also the first American all-metal production fighter. Even so, the open cockpit and fixed landing gear meant it soon became an anachronism. By the late 1930s, more advanced pursuit aircraft were entering service with the Army, with an enclosed cockpit and retractable undercarriage. The Navy continued to operate biplane fighters from its aircraft carriers throughout the decade.

The prospect of another war in Europe created the political impetus to expand and renew American air power. Although separated from Europe by the Atlantic Ocean, it was clear that the United States could be drawn into any conflict on the Continent. The Munich Crisis, which ended in September 1938 with The Sudetenland ceded from Czechoslovakia to Germany, prompted plans to increase the size of the US Army Air Corps. On April 3, 1939, Congress authorized appropriations for an Air Corps of up to 6,000 aircraft. At the time, the service had around 2,200 aircraft, while the US Navy and Marines had a total inventory of 2,100. By the time war was declared in Europe, the United States had already started to build up its air power.

BOEING P-12E

A total of 366 Boeing P-12s of seven different variants were built for the US Army Air Corps between 1929 and 1932, while six other designations were used for engine and airframe test beds. The family was the final biplane fighter for the service and was flown in secondary roles until just after the entry of the United States into World War Two. The last variants to enter service were members of the Model 234 family, which introduced a new semi-monocoque metal fuselage, with raised rear decking, and redesigned tail surfaces. The most numerous version of the Model 234 was the P-12E, 110 of which were delivered to the US Army Air Corps between September 19 and October 15, 1931. The "prototype" of the P-12E (and F4B-3) was a Boeing-owned airframe, the Model 218 (XP-925), which first flew on September 29, 1930. Among the units that flew P-12Es was the 27th Pursuit Squadron (to which "33" was assigned) of the 1st Pursuit Group, based at Selfridge Field in Michigan. The squadron operated P-12 variants from 1930 into 1934. In addition to becoming the standard Army pursuit ship from the late 1920s, the US Navy and Marines received 187 similar F4Bs of four different models, while other variants included the Models 100 (eight), 256 (14) and 267 (nine), of which the last two were produced for Brazil. Delivery of the 586th and last of the family (a F4B-4) occurred in late February 1933.

BELL FM-1 AIRACUDA

The first aircraft from Bell of Buffalo, New York, the FM-1 Airacuda was conceived out of the 1930s' fashion for heavy "strategic fighters" able to escort bombers into enemy territory, intercept bombers at long range, and carry out ground-attack missions. With the partial exception of the Messerschmitt Bf 110, none of these aircraft was successful, and the Airacuda never saw combat. The XFM-1 flew in September 1937 and was followed by nine YFM-1s and three YFM-1As, the latter featuring a tricycle undercarriage. The designation came from "Fighter, Multiplace," and the Airacuda was the only aircraft in this category. The nacelles housed two 37mm (1.46in) Madsen M4 cannon, a powerful weapon, but only fitted with a five-round magazine. A crewman in each nacelle reloaded the guns, while aiming and firing was the responsibility of the copilot in the rear main cockpit. The 1,090hp (813kW) Allison V-1710-41 engines were mounted in pusher configuration and were impossible to keep cool – they frequently overheated on the ground. An emergency bail out would have required feathering both propellers. Failure of the separate gas-powered auxiliary power unit would cause complete shutdown of hydraulic and electrical systems. The Airacudas were briefly organized into a squadron but then dispersed to bases around the US, where they were mainly used to give senior pilots something unusual to fly.

NORTH AMERICAN O-47

Developed by General Aviation, a subsidiary of North American Aviation (NAA), the GA-15 three-seat observation aircraft flew in November 1935 at Dundalk, Maryland. Ordered as the O-47, all production took place at NAA's new factory opened at Inglewood, California, in January 1936. The O-47A used a 975hp (727kW) Wright R-1820-49 Cyclone, and the O-47B a 1,060hp (790kW) R-1820-57 with additional fuel capacity. A total of 239 O-47s were built, but the aircraft never received an official name. It was a rather ungainly looking machine, which featured a position for a photographer/observer lying prone in the belly. During maneuvers before the war, it was determined that light observation aircraft like the Piper L-4 Cub were more effective cooperating with ground troops. The O-47 was also a large, steady target and, with a top speed of 221mph (356km/h), could not escape an air attack. Variants of fighters such as the F-4 (Lockheed P-38 Lightning) and F-6 (North American P-51 Mustang) would later be developed for the tactical photoreconnaissance mission. Some O-47s were used overseas in the early part of the war, but most were relegated to secondary roles such as target towing and anti-submarine patrol.

NORTHROP A-17A

Northrop's Gamma transport formed the basis of the A-13 attack aircraft, of which 110 were ordered in 1934. The prototype was designated XA-16 and, during trials, proved to be overpowered, an unusual problem for a military aircraft in the 1930s. The 800hp (597kW) Pratt & Whitney R-1830-7 was replaced with a 750hp (560kW) R-1535-11 on the A-17, which entered service in August 1935. Ironically, the last 129 built, as A-17As, had 850hp (634kW) R-1535-13s. They also had a fully enclosed landing gear, rather than the semi-recessed units of the A-17. Most of these aircraft had short US Army Air Corps careers, being returned to the manufacturer for onward sale to Britain and France, where the need for any type of modern combat aircraft in June 1940 was greater. This image shows at least 16 A-17As, with their US markings stripped off, awaiting delivery back to the factory from an army airfield in the Midwest. In the end, the aircraft were too late to be used by the French, while the British dispatched 60 of the 93 Nomad Mk 1s (British designation) they received to the South African Air Force as trainers. Douglas continued offering the design for export, and some of the aircraft were powered by 1,200hp (895kW) R-1820-87 engines. A batch of 34 for Peru was commandeered by the US Army Air Forces in 1942 as the A-33.

CURTISS A-18 SHRIKE

In 1931–32, Curtiss-Wright built a series of attack aircraft for the US Army Air Corps: the A-8, A-10 and A-12, all named Shrike. They were heavy and ungainly single-engined monoplanes with externally braced wings and fixed landing gear; their main concession to modernity was enclosed cockpits for the crew. Although quickly obsolescent, some were still in service in December 1941. Designed by Don Berlin, who was behind several successful Northrop aircraft, the XA-14 of 1934 was a much sleeker design, sharing only the name and the attack role with the earlier Shrikes. The twin-engined, two-seat aircraft was initially tested with two Curtiss XR-1510 twin-row radials, before being re-engined with 735hp (548kW) Wright R-1670-5s. The 13 service test aircraft, designated Y1A-18s, were fitted with 600hp (448kW) Wright R-1820-47s. The new Shrikes were purchased for US$104,640 apiece, about five times that of the A-12. The A-18s were issued to the 8th Attack Squadron, 3rd Attack Group, at Barksdale, Louisiana, but no further production order was placed. They suffered from a weak landing gear and eight aircraft suffered from collapses while in service. The last examples were used in the Panama Canal Zone in 1942.

MARTIN B-10

Built as a private venture, the Martin B-10 was faster than contemporary fighters when it first flew in February 1932. Its modern features included an enclosed gun turret, retractable undercarriage, and all-metal structure. The maximum bombload was 2,260lb (1,025kg), typically comprising four 600lb (272kg) weapons, seen here falling from a formation of B-10Bs, the main production version, which equipped five bombardment groups. The B-10B had 775hp (578kW) Wright R-1820-33 engines, while the B-12A was a variant with 700hp (521kW) Pratt & Whitney Hornets. A few of the 34 built were operated on floats for coastal patrol. A total of 153 B-10s and B-12s were built for the US Army Air Corps and a further 189 for export customers, including Siam, Turkey, China, and the Netherlands East Indies. The last acquired 116 examples and used them in combat during the first months of the Pacific War. In January 1934, the US Army Air Corps decided to standardize light blue fuselages for both tactical and training types. It took a while for all aircraft in the inventory to be repainted, but new ones, such as the B-10Bs ordered that year, were delivered in blue, while B-10s from previous orders were Olive Drab. A few B-10Bs remained in service when Japan attacked the Philippines in December 1941.

DOUGLAS B-18 BOLO

In early 1934, the Air Corps issued a requirement for a replacement for its Martin B-10 bombers. The new aircraft was to be able to carry twice as much, twice as far. Martin responded with its Model 146, which was essentially a B-10 with a wider fuselage; Boeing offered the four-engined Model 299; and Douglas the DB-1, which first flew in April 1935. This was essentially the wings and tail of a DC-2 airliner married to a new fuselage containing a bomb bay and three gun positions. The Martin was rejected, and the Boeing 299 evolved into the B-17, but the DB-1 was ordered immediately as the B-18 Bolo, a contract for 133 being signed in January 1936. The last example of this batch was modified with a nose turret as the DB-2, but this configuration was not adopted. A revised nose with the bombardier's position extended forward was standard on the 177 B-18As. The Douglas factory at Santa Monica, California, built all 370 Bolos, with B-18As rolling off the line from April 1938. This view of the Douglas ramp shows B-18As awaiting delivery to the US Army Air Corps, which operated them within four bombardment groups and two reconnaissance squadrons. Many would later become radar-equipped B-18Bs used for anti-submarine patrols.

GRUMMAN F2F

The next step in the evolution of Grumman fighters was the F2F, which flew in October 1933, with deliveries to the Navy beginning in early 1935. With one seat rather than two, it had a shorter body than the FF, with a metal fuselage and fabric-covered wings. The F2F-1 was built in sufficient quantities to equip two of the four existing carrier air groups, those of USS *Ranger* and *Lexington*. Within these groups, each aircraft had a place in a strict hierarchy, denoted by the fuselage code letters, but also the arrangement of color on the aircraft. When F2F-1 BuNo 9624 was photographed in the winter of 1938, the lemon-yellow tail surfaces indicated assignment to the *Lexington's* air group; the code "2-F-1" marked it as the first aircraft of Fighting Squadron Two (VF-2B), whose color was red; and the fully colored engine cowling distinguished it as a section leader. The second (right wing) aircraft in a section would have half the upper half of the cowling in the squadron color, and the third (left wing) aircraft, the lower half. This system made getting into formation after take-off and after combat much easier but relied on all aircraft being serviceable and was somewhat inflexible.

GRUMMAN F3F

To improve its stability, Grumman stretched the F2F fuselage and added longer wings. The XF3F-1 first flew in this new form in May 1935, followed by 54 production F3F-1s with the 650hp (485kW) Pratt & Whitney Twin Wasp and 81 F3F-2s with 950hp (709kW) Wright R-1820-22s. The F3F-2s were mainly assigned to land-based US Marine Corps squadrons and to the Enterprise Air Group. Fighter squadron VF-6 began the transition from the Boeing F4B-4 to the F3F-2 in December 1937, and here the first and second sections line up in the correct order for the camera. Squadron designations changed frequently in this period as they moved between air groups, and new carriers entered the fleet. The 6 matched CV-6, USS *Enterprise*'s pennant number, and was shared across the fighter, bomber, torpedo, and other squadrons (VF-6, VB-6, VT-6, etc.). For a time, a B suffix was added to squadron designators to indicate assignment to the Battle Fleet and an S for the Scouting Fleet. Fighting Six operated the F3F until 1940, when it transitioned to the Grumman F4F-3 Wildcat. The last F3F-2s were retired by the Marines in October 1941.

GREAT LAKES XB2G-1

In 1933, the US Navy issued a requirement for a two-seat dive-bomber capable of carrying a 1,000lb (454kg) bomb. Great Lakes Aircraft of Cleveland, Ohio, replied with a single-engined biplane, powered by a 750hp (560kW) Pratt & Whitney R-1535-64 engine, with a fixed undercarriage. Great Lakes was mainly known for its light aircraft but had assembled Martin T4M torpedo bombers under license. In a mid-1933 evaluation against the Consolidated XB2Y-1, also an open-cockpit fixed-gear biplane, the XBG-1 proved superior, and 60 were built as BG-1s, with enclosed cockpits. From October 1934, they served with one squadron that deployed on carriers USS *Ranger* and *Lexington,* and with two Marine Corps squadrons from 1935-40. Although the basic design was approaching obsolescence, in 1936 Great Lakes tried to secure more sales by modernizing the BG-1 with such fashionable features as a retractable undercarriage and enclosed bomb bay. These gave the XB2G-1 a portly appearance, evident in this image of the pilot running up the Wasp Junior engine, while the observer finishes his cigarette. The type did not progress beyond a single prototype, BuNo 9722, which was assigned to the US Marine Corps headquarters as a utility aircraft. The BG-1 was the last Great Lakes design to enter production.

NORTHROP BT-1

Northrop, then a subsidiary of Douglas, successfully bid for a US Navy requirement for a carrier-based dive-bomber with the XBT-1, designed by Edward Heinemann. A total of 54 were ordered in September 1936, powered by 825hp (615kW) Pratt & Whitney R-1534-95 Twin Wasp Junior engines. The wheels retracted into fairings and a multi-part canopy covered the pilot and observer, who manned a single 0.30in (7.62mm) machine gun. The pilot had a 0.50in (12.7mm) gun firing through the propeller arc, while a 1,000lb (454kg) bomb could be carried on an under-fuselage cradle and two 100lb (45kg) bombs under the wings. During tests, it was found that deploying the large split dive brakes caused excessive buffeting of the tail section. National Advisory Committee for Aeronautics (NACA) suggested perforating the brakes and this cured the problem. The same design would be used on the Douglas SBD Dauntless and a variation of it on the Curtiss SB2C Helldiver. The XBT-2 was a modified BT-1 with a fully retracting landing gear, a revised canopy, and an 800 hp (597kW) Wright XR-1820-32 engine. First flown in April 1938, it became the basis of the SBD-1 Dauntless, the most successful Allied naval dive-bomber of the war. Before long, large numbers of SBDs were rolling off the El Segundo production line (now absorbed by Douglas as Northrop went its own way) and BT-1s were relegated to training duties. This gaggle of BT-1s over Miami, Florida, in late 1939 belong to the Naval Air Operational Training Command (NAOTC).

GRUMMAN JF-2

Grumman's Model G-7 was the first Navy aircraft acquired under the new general utility category, designated by the letter J. The XJF-1 amphibian completed its maiden flight in April 1933, and 27 JF-1s were ordered for the Navy after evaluation. It only received the official name Duck in 1940. An initial requirement to be catapulted from large warships was dropped and the JFs were operated from aircraft carriers and land bases. Powered by a 700hp (522kW) R-1535-62 Twin Wasp Junior, the JF-1s represented a huge leap in performance over the Loening OL-1s they replaced, which also had a large single float. The main wheels retracted into the float in a similar way to Grumman's fighters. A passenger or stretcher case could be carried inside the fuselage and sometimes a radio operator squeezed in alongside the observer. From October 1934 to November 1935, 15 JF-2s were delivered to the US Coast Guard at eight bases. No fewer than eight were assigned to Cape May, New Jersey; all the other stations had a single aircraft. Four aircraft were traded to the Navy in 1941 but five later J2F-5 and -6 versions were acquired in 1942–45. In 1942, to enable Grumman to concentrate on fighters and torpedo bombers, production was transferred to Columbia Aircraft, also based on Long Island, New York.

CONSOLIDATED XPB2Y-1 CORONADO

Named Coronado after the peninsula opposite San Diego in California, the XPB2Y-1 flying boat first flew in December 1937. Stability issues on its maiden flight led to the addition of mid-span fins on the tailplane, as seen here, by the time of its fourth flight in February 1938. These did not solve the problem and the whole tail was subsequently rebuilt, removing the central fin and fitting Liberator-style endplate fins on a tailplane with strong dihedral. Navy evaluation from August 1938 led to an order for six PB2Y-Is the following March. Production problems delayed delivery to the Navy until December 1940. Between prototype and production, the hull was also redesigned, and the series aircraft were very different from the XPB2Y-1. Some had nose, ventral, and tail turrets and were operated as patrol bombers, but the capacious fuselage made it more useful as a transport or ambulance aircraft. Heavier weights threw up spray that corroded the inboard three-bladed aluminum propellers, so four-bladed steel props were substituted on the inner engines of later variants. The prototype itself was repainted in overall blue and given the name *Blue Goose*. Between 1943 and 1945, it was used as a VIP transport carrying various dignitaries, including Admiral Chester Nimitz, between Hawaii and the mainland. The flying boat was scrapped at Naval Air Station (NAS) North Island in August 1945.

SEVERSKY BT-8

Russian émigré Alexander de Seversky founded the Seversky Aircraft Corporation in 1931. One of its first designs was the float-equipped SEV-3, which set several records for amphibian aircraft. Modified with a fixed wheel undercarriage, it emerged victorious from an evaluation against the North American NA-16 in 1935, resulting in an order for 30 as BT-8s. It was the first US Army Air Corps basic trainer designed as such from the outset, rather than being converted from an observation aircraft or modified from a primary trainer. Innovations included sliding canopies and split trailing-edge flaps. Unfortunately, it was also fairly expensive, tricky to fly – with poor stall characteristics – and difficult to maintain. The government provided the 400hp (298kW) Pratt & Whitney R-985-11 Wasp Junior engine for the aircraft, which was barely adequate, although an improvement on the 350hp (261kW) R-975 that powered the prototype. The BT-8s were operated from Randolph Field, Texas. North American continued to revise the NA-16 and the resulting NA-19 was better than the BT-8 on all counts, leading to the Air Corps eventually buying more than 600 NA-19s as the BT-9. Blue and yellow began to appear on trainers from about 1930. After 1934, it was adopted by all Air Corps aircraft as a means of ensuring maximum visibility in the air as a safety measure, as well as saving money on paint.

NORTH AMERICAN AT-6A TEXAN

The main advanced trainer of American, British, and Commonwealth forces of World War Two, the North American AT-6 Texan was derived from the BC-1 basic combat trainer of 1938, which itself owed much to the earlier BT-9 basic trainer. The BT-9 had fixed landing gear and a 400hp (298kW) Wright R-975-7, giving it a top speed of 170mph (274km/h). The AT-6A, with a retractable gear, was around 35mph (56km/h) faster powered by a 550hp (410kW) Pratt & Whitney R-1340. The prototype was built at Dundalk, Maryland, but production took place at Inglewood in California, and then Dallas, with the former plant building 637 and its Texan counterpart assembling 588 AT-6As (some of which are seen here). Noorduyn Aviation in Canada built 1,500 more for the US Army Air Forces and 1,173 Harvard Mk Is, mainly for the British Commonwealth Air Training Plan. A shortage of some alloys led to the AT-6C using plywood for the rear fuselage and tail, but subsequent versions reverted to metal construction. From April 1941, it was ordered that advanced trainers should be delivered in unpainted aluminum, as illustrated by this line of AT-6As awaiting delivery, wearing the national insignia used from August 1919 to May 1942. A total of 15,495 T-6s and Navy SNJs (scout trainers) were built at an average cost of US$24,952, with the last ordered in 1952.

RYAN PT-16

With NAS North Island and its carrier piers in the background, student pilots line up for inspection in front of their shiny PT-16 primary trainers at Lindbergh Field in San Diego, California, probably in late 1939. The Ryan School of Aeronautics was founded in June 1931. Owner T. Claude Ryan had long sold his stake in the Ryan Airline business, which was famous for building the *Spirit of St. Louis*. In 1934, he started a new Ryan Aeronautical Company, of which the school eventually became a subsidiary. Its first aircraft was the ST, a high-performance civilian trainer, powered by a 125hp (93kW) Menasco L-365-1. The fixed-undercarriage trainer was of mostly metal construction with open cockpits and external bracing for the wings. It had a maximum speed of 128mph (206km/h). The US Army Air Corps procured an STA-1 for evaluation in 1939 as the XPT-16, followed by 15 YPT-16s, which were evaluated at the Ryan School. An order for 20 similar PT-20s followed. The 100 PT-21s were powered by a 132hp (98kW) Kinner R-440 radial, and the 1,023 PT-22s with a 160hp (119kW) Kinner R-540-1. They were operated by civilian-operated schools, including Ryan's own establishments at San Diego and Tucson.

VULTEE BT-13 VALIANT

The Vultee V-54 of 1938 shared the designer and many features of the Hughes H-1 racer. It was considered to be too sophisticated for the basic training role, so Vultee developed a simpler aircraft with a fixed landing gear and two-position propeller instead. This was accepted by the US Army Air Corps in September 1939 as the BT-13 Valiant, becoming the subject of the largest order at that point, covering 300 aircraft. The BT-13 had a 450hp (336kW) Pratt & Whitney R-985 engine, an enclosed cockpit, dual controls, flaps, and a radio. The BT-13 became the most numerous basic trainer ever built, with 11,537 produced up to the summer of 1944. Over 1,300 were allocated to the navy as SNV-1s. The blue and yellow scheme for trainers was replaced by aluminum from April 1941 and the red center in the national insignia was eliminated from June 1942, giving an approximate timeframe for this image of BT-13s lined up at the Vultee plant at Downey, California. Vultee merged with Consolidated in 1942. Consolidated-Vultee built 30,903 B-24s, PBYs, and BT-13 trainers during the war, the second-largest quantity after North American Aviation. The Downey factory was taken over by North American in 1948 and later became an important site for NASA's manned spacecraft program.

FAIRCHILD F24

Fairchild's Model 22 was flown in 1932 as a two-seat civilian light plane and around 200 had been sold by 1935. Its success led to the four-seat Model 24, powered by either a 145hp (108kW) Warner (as F24W) radial or similarly rated Ranger inline engine (F24R). Construction was fabric over aluminum tube and wood. The US Coast Guard became the first military operator, acquiring two J2K-1s and two J2K-2s, which were civilian F24Rs, commissioning them in March and May 1937. Two were assigned to St. Petersburg, Florida, and two to Charleston, South Carolina, for utility and observation missions. Unfortunately, all four had been written-off in accidents by May 1941, with J2K-1 V160 crashing in August 1940. A further 13 were bought by the Navy as GK-1s from 1941. While several Fairchild 24s fly today in US Coast Guard color schemes, none originally served with the military branch. From 1941, the Army purchased 163 Warner-engined aircraft as UC-61 Forwarders but transferred most of them to the United Kingdom, where they were named Argus. In total, over 600 were used by the RAF and Air Transport Auxiliary, including 306 Argus Mk IIIs (UC-61Ks) with Ranger L-440-7 engines. The US Army Air Force did use 148 UC-61As, plus impressed civilian Model 24s.

BEECHCRAFT C-43

The Beechcraft D17 was designed as one of the first executive aircraft, able to fly four businessmen in considerable comfort. The mounting of the upper wing aft of the lower one gave improved visibility and led to the name Staggerwing. Flying in November 1932, sales were initially slow for this expensive aircraft in the Great Depression, but over 400 D17s had been sold by the outbreak of war. In 1939, the US Army Air Corps acquired three for evaluation as the C-43 and, from 1941, took 270 more UC-43 Traveler utility transports, plus large numbers bought from private owners. The Navy took nine ex-civilian aircraft and bought 352 from Beech as the GB-2. The YC-43s were issued to the air attachés of the US embassies in Rome, Paris, and London, with 39-139, seen here serving Brigadier General Martin F. Scanlon, mainly flying from Hatfield and Hendon north of London. In 1941, it was transferred to the RAF as Traveller Mk I DR628. The RAF flew 20 Travellers, mostly in the Middle East, and the Fleet Air Arm had 75 for communications duties in the UK. This example later had many civilian owners in Africa, the United States, and Europe, and still flies today in its original color scheme as N295BS in the Netherlands.

CHAPTER 7

AMERICAN AIR POWER UNCHAINED

INTRODUCTION

The growth of America's aviation industry during World War Two was one of the most impressive feats of the conflict. In a few short years output increased dramatically.

Between July 1940 and August 1945, the Unites States built 295,959 aircraft, of which 158,880 went to the US Army Air Forces and 73,711 to the US Navy and Marine Corps. The "arsenal of democracy" also supplied 38,811 aircraft to the British Empire and Commonwealth, and another 14,717 to the Soviet Union.

Production concentrated on relatively few primary combat aircraft, with multiple sites being established for important types. The tremendous build up of manufacturing capacity during the conflict saw the number of aircraft rolling off the assembly lines more than double between 1941 and 1942 and again in 1943, reaching a peak of 96,270 aircraft built in 1944 alone. Production during the first seven months of 1945 nearly equaled the total output for the whole of 1942. Around two-thirds of the aircraft built in the United States during the war were combat designs, the other third transports, trainers, or communication types. American aircraft fought in all theaters of the war.

CONSOLIDATED B-24 LIBERATOR

The assembly line at Consolidated's plant at Lindbergh Field, San Diego, where 7,034 Liberators were produced, including almost all the 2,696 B-24Ds and derivatives, such as the PB4Y-1s for the US Navy, seen here in sea search camouflage. The San Diego factory was originally intended to be a secondary line for the Boeing B-17 Flying Fortress until Consolidated's chief engineer proposed a new bomber built around a new high-lift wing designed by David R. Davis. The "Davis Wing" gave the B-24 greater range and more carrying capacity over a longer distance than the B-17, although its actual maximum weight and bombload were lower. The XB-24 first flew on March 30, 1939, but the B-24D, the first truly combat-capable variant, was not delivered until early 1942. It featured powered dorsal and tail turrets, while a ventral ball turret was added during the production run. Powered nose turrets were introduced with the B-24H and gave much needed improved frontal protection. The original San Diego factory was joined by plants at Fort Worth, Texas, Willow Run, Michigan, and Tulsa, Oklahoma, with the last two operated by Ford and Douglas, respectively. Together they delivered 18,493 Liberators, making it the most produced bomber and American military aircraft ever.

BOEING B-17 FLYING FORTRESS

Flying Fortresses of the 390th Bomb Group drop 260lb (118kg) M81 fragmentation bombs above cloud. B-17F 42-3312 *Sequatchiee* in the foreground was delivered from the Douglas plant in Tulsa, Oklahoma, on May 5, 1943, to Cheyenne, Wyoming, for modification to the latest combat standard. It was assigned to the 570th Bomb Squadron at Framingham in Suffolk on July 14. On a mission to Duren on October 20, it was hit by flak and turned back. Four crewmen bailed out over the sea and were lost, although the bomber returned to base. On June 22, 1944, flak knocked out an engine and *Sequatchiee* crashed near Dreux in France. Four of the crew became prisoners of war, and five evaded capture with the help of the locals; two were later betrayed to the Gestapo and shot. The B-17 was the most famous wartime US bomber. A journalist described it as a "flying fortress" before the first flight on July 28, 1935, and the name stuck, although the prototype was lightly armed compared to later models such as the B-17G, which sported up to 13 defensive machine guns. From February 1944, B-17s began to arrive in the UK in natural metal finish, saving the weight of the paint and speeding up construction, although camouflaged aircraft served until the war's end.

BOEING B-29 SUPERFORTRESS

The dominant image of the B-29 Superfortress is a highly polished airframe gleaming in the Pacific sun, but the XB-29, which first flew on September 21, 1942, and the first aircraft off the production line were delivered in the standard Olive Drab and neutral grey scheme. One camouflaged YB-29 was sent to the UK in March 1944, staying for two months. Although the Superfortress never saw combat in Europe, the visit allowed 8th Air Force staff to familiarize themselves with the aircraft and to mislead German intelligence that the B-29 would soon be deployed there. Many technical issues, particularly with the Wright R-3350 Duplex Cyclone engines, delayed the type's combat debut until May 1944, when B-29s first bombed Japan from bases in India. To support these missions over the Himalayan mountains (known as the "Hump"), fuel and bombs had to be pre-positioned at Chinese bases as the distance was too far for fully laden B-29s. This aircraft, 42-6242, photographed over the US, was issued to the 468th Bombardment Group at Kharagpur, India. Declared "war weary," it was stripped of its gun turrets and converted to a bulk fuel tanker and was named *Esso Express*. It hauled gasoline on 1,200-mile (1,931km) missions to Pengsham, China, where B-29 bombers would refuel on missions to Japan.

LOCKHEED HUDSON

The Hudson was derived from the Model 14 Super Electra, which Lockheed mocked-up into a bomber for a British purchasing commission in early 1938. Compared to this airliner, the Hudson Mk I had a glazed nose cone for bomb aiming, twin 0.303in (7.7mm) machine guns fixed in front of the cockpit, and a bomb bay with capacity for 3,300lb (1,497kg) of bombs or depth charges. This example, N7306, was probably photographed after delivery to the UK, but before the Boulton Paul dorsal turret was fitted. The US Army Air Forces used a few, mainly as gunnery trainers, but Britain ordered an initial 200 and issued most of them to Coastal Command for patrol, anti-submarine, and search and rescue duties. They occasionally flew bomber missions over Europe but were not best suited to the role. The Hudson Mk I entered service in May 1939 with No. 224 Squadron at Leuchars, Fife, and N7306 was serving with that unit on April 14, 1940, when it encountered a Luftwaffe Heinkel He 115 during a patrol to Stavanger, Norway. The floatplane's crew called in backup, and a pair of Messerschmitt Bf 109E fighters attacked. The Hudson was shot down near Sola, and the crew were declared missing, presumed dead.

MARTIN 187 BALTIMORE MK I

Brightly polished first Baltimore Mk I NXM43 sits outside the Martin Factory at Middle River, Maryland, on June 15, 1941, with a row of B-26 Marauders behind. The Model 187 Baltimore was a development of the Model 167 and both types were built solely for export customers. All but a few of France's Model 167s were taken over by the RAF as the Maryland, with some also serving with South African Air Force (SAAF) squadrons. NXM43 was delivered to the UK as AG685 in October 1941 for evaluation at Boscombe Down, Wiltshire. The Baltimore was characterized, like its predecessor, by a very narrow fuselage, but one that was deeper and was not blocked by bulkheads, enabling better communication between crew members. Powered by two Wright R-2600 Cyclones of 1,660hp (1,238kW) and able to carry a 2,000lb (907kg) payload, the Baltimore was an effective light bomber, serving with eight RAF and three SAAF squadrons. There were several marks, differing mainly in defensive armament, with the Mk I having a single Vickers machine gun, and later variants powered twin-gun turrets. All operational examples served in the Western Desert and then Italy. With 1,175 built up to May 1944, it was Martin's second-most produced design after the Marauder. No complete examples survive today.

DOUGLAS A-20G HAVOC

Jack Northrop and Edward Heinemann created the twin-engined Douglas Model 7 in 1938 to a broad US Army requirement for an attack bomber. It was ordered by France even before the US Army Air Corps accepted it in early 1940 as the A-20 Havoc, quickly followed by the RAF, with which it was known as the Boston. The British used the aircraft as a day bomber and a night fighter, as well as operating them in the intruder role. The first US bombing raid on Europe was carried out on July 4, 1942, by American pilots flying Bostons borrowed from the RAF. The Soviet Union received over 3,000 of the 7,478 A-20s built, and the RAF had 1,800. US A-20s were widely used in Europe, North Africa, and the Pacific. The late-model A-20G replaced the bombardier's position with a solid gun nose containing up to four 0.50in (12.7mm) machine guns and two 20mm (0.787in) cannon. Carrying the "last two" of the serial on the nose and tail, A-20G 42-86657 was flown by the 409th Bombardment Group while in training at Pounds Field in Tyler, Texas. The group embarked for England in February 1944 and, assigned to 9th Air Force, took part in the build-up to D-Day, and in the subsequent campaigns, moving to France in August. By the end of the year, the 406th had converted to the A-26 Invader, Douglas' successor to the A-20.

NORTH AMERICAN B-25 MITCHELL

The most important US medium bomber of the war, the Mitchell was made famous by the "Doolittle Raid" of April 1942, when 16 B-25Cs flew off the carrier USS *Hornet* to bomb targets in Japan. The prototype had flown in August 1940 and soon large numbers were on the order books. B-25s were built in factories at Inglewood, California, and Kansas City, Kansas, with all B-25J models assembled at the latter location. The B-25J was well defended with 0.50in (12.7mm) machine guns in nose, waist, and tail positions and in a top turret. Some, including this example, were fitted with "package guns" in blisters under the cockpit, fired by the pilot. Other modifications, first developed in the combat zone, replaced the bombardier's position with a four- or six-gun nose to create specialized strafers. Further developments saw the B-25G and H models sporting a 75mm (2.95in) cannon in the nose for anti-shipping attacks. The B-25H had 15 guns in total, plus capacity for 3,200lb (1,451kg) of bombs. Mitchells were used by the US Army Air Forces in most war theaters except northwest Europe, although the RAF's 2nd Tactical Air Force did fly significant numbers in support of the Normandy invasion and subsequent campaigns.

CURTISS P-40 WARHAWK

The XP-40 Hawk first flew in October 1938 and was developed from earlier radial-engined Curtiss Hawk monoplanes. The P-40, often known by its British names, Tomahawk, Kittyhawk, or Warhawk, was the US Army Air Force's primary fighter when America joined the war in late 1941. Surpassed by more modern and powerful fighters such as the Lockheed P-38 Lightning, Republic P-47 Thunderbolt, and North American P-51 Mustang, it was largely relegated to second-line duties by 1943, when this photo of P-40Fs serving with 504th Single Engine Flying Training Squadron of the Army Air Forces Pilot School was taken. Accidents in training were common and the second Warhawk in this formation, 41-14180, was written-off at Moore Field, Texas, on November 2, 1943, when it stalled and spun in after take-off. Although most P-40s were powered by some version of the Allison V-1710, the P-40F and P-40L used the Packard-built Rolls-Royce V-1650 Merlin. While this engine was heavier, its greater power increased maximum speed from the P-40E's 354mph (570km/h) to 373mph (600km/h). To counter instability, later P-40Fs had longer fuselages and higher weights, which somewhat reduced the speed differential. There were just over 2,000 Merlin-engined P-40s out of a total production of 16,802 up to 1944.

LOCKHEED P-38 LIGHTNING

Although often overshadowed by the North American P-51 Mustang, the P-38 was the fighter flown by America's top aces. The Lightning first flew in January 1939 and remained in production until 1945, with just over 10,000 built by Lockheed in Burbank, California. The most numerous version was the P-38J, fitted with 1,610hp (1,201kW) Allison V-1710-89/91 engines, and flaps that could be extended in a dive to prevent loss of pitch control as speed built up. This particular P-38J, 42-68008, was used as a company demonstrator. In February 1944, Tony LeVier took it to England and toured 8th Air Force bases, naming it *Snafuperman*, after a cartoon about a bumbling soldier (Private Snafu) who gains superpowers. At the time, the accident rate in Lightning units had become unacceptably high and pilots were losing faith in the aircraft. LeVier flew many aerobatic demonstrations with one propeller feathered, proving that the Lightning was fully controllable even on one engine, and showed off the new dive flaps, which allowed pullouts at high speed. In May, it was decided to convert P-38 groups to the P-51 and those P-38Js that reached Europe were diverted to 9th and 15th Air Forces. The P-38J and later variants had greater success in the Pacific Theater, where combat was usually at a lower altitude, and long-range was more important.

NORTH AMERICAN P-51 MUSTANG

Often regarded as the best production fighter of the war, the P-51 Mustang was built to a British requirement and went from drawing board to first flight in 117 days, the prototype first flying on October 26, 1942, with an Allison V-1710 engine. The RAF was disappointed with the high-altitude performance of its Mustang Mk Is and fitted supercharged Rolls-Royce Merlin 60s in ten test aircraft. This led to the P-51B and C (built in Los Angeles and Dallas, respectively) with Packard-built Merlins, which entered combat service in late 1943. Seen on a test flight over the US, this P-51B was allocated to the RAF as FX883, a Mustang Mk III, but never actually served with the British. It was returned to the US Army Air Forces in December 1943 as 43-12372 and was issued to the 354th Fighter Group of 9th Air Force. On February 21, 1944, it was shot down in combat with a Focke-Wulf Fw 190 near Brunswick, the pilot being killed. The P-51D with a bubble canopy was actually slower than the B/C versions, but had additional fuel capacity and six, rather than four, 0.50in (12.7mm) machine guns in the wings. With underwing fuel tanks, the P-51D could escort bombers all the way from England to Berlin.

REPUBLIC P-47 THUNDERBOLT

A gaggle of factory-fresh P-47D Thunderbolts flying over Long Island, New York, near Farmingdale, the main manufacturing site for Republic Aircraft. Farmingdale, along with plants at Evansville, Indiana, and a Curtiss factory in Buffalo, New York, were delivering 660 Thunderbolts a month by late 1943. With a final total of 15,660 produced, the P-47 was the most numerous American fighter ever. It was also the largest single-engined fighter of the war, powered by a 2,000hp (1,491kW) Pratt & Whitney R-2800-59 radial and armed with eight 0.50in (12.7mm) machine guns in the wings. From the P-47D-25 production block onwards, Thunderbolts had a cut down rear fuselage and a "bubble top" clear canopy, greatly improving rearward vision. The Thunderbolt in the foreground, 42-26428, was soon sent to the frontline, issued to the 8th Air Force's 353rd Fighter Group (FG) at Raydon, Suffolk, and then to the 356th FG at nearby Martlesham Heath. It was then transferred to the 354th FG of 9th Air Force, which was tasked with the tactical support of Allied troops in Europe and changed bases as the front line moved. On January 16, 1945, it was shot down by antiaircraft fire and crashed in Luxembourg, the pilot being killed.

BELL P-63 KINGCOBRA

Bell's P-39 Airacobra and P-63 Kingcobra were unusual in having a tricycle undercarriage and the engine mounted in the fuselage, driving a propeller via a long shaft that ran under the cockpit. This enabled the nose to be used for armament, which was either a 20mm or 37mm (0.787 or 1.46in) cannon, depending on the variant. The Airacobra was obsolescent by 1941, although many were supplied to the Soviet Union, where they were used effectively, mainly in the ground-support role. The P-63 Kingcobra was designed as a development of the P-39 with low-drag laminar-flow wings, an Allison V-1710-93 engine of 1,325hp (989kW), and better armament, including 0.50in (12.7mm) machine guns in the nose and underwing pods. Pylons on the wings enabled carriage of bombs. The XP-63 first flew on December 7, 1942, and this P-63A was used for development work at Wright Field, Ohio. Notably, between September 1944 and March 1945, it was used to determine the type's performance at war emergency (boosted) power. These studies were somewhat academic as the war was nearing its end, and the US services never adopted the Kingcobra as frontline equipment. The Soviet Union was the recipient of the majority of the 1,726 P-63As produced.

BELL XP-77

In between the P-39 and P-63, Bell developed the diminutive XP-77, which was an early configuration for the Airacobra dusted off and redesigned to use non-strategic materials, mainly wood. Like its bigger brothers, it had a tricycle undercarriage, but the engine, a 520hp (388kW) Ranger XV-770, was mounted in a conventional position in the nose. The pilot had good visibility in all directions except forward, where it was largely blocked by the long nose. Weighing only 3,583lb (1,625kg) with pilot and fuel aboard, it had a top speed of 330mph (53lkm/h), but this would have been much reduced when armor and guns were added. A supercharged version of the V-770 engine never materialized. The P-77 only made sense as a point defense interceptor to guard vital targets. Only two of six planned prototypes were built and the first was delivered only six months after the contract was signed. The initial XP-77 first flew in April 1944 and proved to have tricky handling characteristics with lower-than-expected performance. The second prototype crashed in October 1944 after entering an inverted spin; the pilot bailed out. The first survives at the National Museum of the US Air Force in Dayton, Ohio.

GRUMMAN F4F WILDCAT

Sharing many common features with the F3F and earlier Grumman biplanes, the XF4F-2 Wildcat first flew in February 1939, although its origin was in an unsuccessful prototype of 1936. Powered by a 1,200hp (805kW) Pratt & Whitney R-1830 nine-cylinder radial, the initial production F4F-3 had four 0.50in (12.7mm) machine guns in the wings, which did not fold. Most F4F-3s went to the Marine Corps for land-based opposition, or to the Fleet Air Arm as the Martlet Mk I. The F4F-4 (Martlet Mk II) had manually folding wings with six guns and was the principal fighter on US carriers in the early part of the war. Here, F4F-4s of VGF-29 share the deck of escort carrier USS Santee with VGS-29 Douglas SBD Dauntlesses during Operation *Torch*, the Allied landings in North Africa in November 1942. *Santee*'s air group saw combat against Vichy French forces around Safi in Morocco. The Wildcats strafed troop columns and the Dauntlesses bombed airfields. In the Pacific, the Wildcat was slightly inferior in performance to the Mitsubishi A6M Zero, but had heavier armament and was better able to survive battle damage. General Motors built Wildcats as the FM-1 and FM-2. The latter had a taller tail fin and four guns. In total, 7,722 Wildcats were produced.

GRUMMAN F6F HELLCAT

Originally conceived as an F4F Wildcat with a 2,000hp engine, the XF6F Hellcat emerged as a considerably larger all-new aircraft, albeit one sharing some visual similarity with its predecessor. The XF6F-1 flew in June 1942 with a 1,500hp (1,119kW) Wright R-2600-10 Twin Cyclone turning a three-bladed Curtiss Electric propeller. The second prototype was fitted with the Pratt & Whitney R-2800-10 Double Wasp and a Hamilton Standard Hydromatic constant-speed propeller, and this was the combination adopted for production. The first prototype was also refitted but it crash-landed less than a month after its first flight with this arrangement. It was rebuilt and flew again as the XF6F-4 with yet another engine, the 2,000hp (1,492kW) R-2800-27. The complicated landing gear door arrangement was discarded before the F6F-3 entered service in early 1943. Various minor refinements produced the F6F-5, production of which amounted to 6,431 out of a total of 12,275 Hellcats. Used mainly in the Pacific, the six-gun Hellcat scored three-quarters of all US Navy air-to-air victories in the war, for a total of just under 5,000. It was also flown by US Marine Corps squadrons and the Fleet Air Arm. Postwar operators included France, Argentina, and Uruguay.

VOUGHT F4U CORSAIR

The Chance-Vought Corporation first flew the XF4U-1 Corsair in May 1940, in response to a 1938 US Navy requirement. Powered by a Pratt & Whitney R-2800 Double Wasp 18-cylinder radial, the Corsair had a distinctive inverted gull wing layout, which helped to keep the large propeller clear of the ground. The initial-production F4U-1, known as the "Birdcage" Corsair for its heavily framed canopy, was rejected by the US Navy for carrier operations because of the poor view for the pilot, and tendency to bounce on landing. Despite these faults, in early 1943, 34 F4U-1s were converted as F4U-2 night-fighters with an APS-4 air-to-air radar in a wing tip pod. This had a range of only 2 miles (3.2km). One of the machine guns was removed on the starboard wing to counteract the extra weight of the radar. Later night-fighter variants, such as the F4U-4N, had four 20mm (0.787in) cannon. Here F4U-2Ns of VF(N)-101, Detachment B, taxi for take-off aboard carrier USS *Intrepid* (CV-11), prior to a raid against the Japanese stronghold of Truk in February 1944. The squadron only scored five confirmed victories, but pioneered carrier night operations and tactics later used more successfully by pilots flying Grumman F6F Hellcat night-fighters.

GRUMMAN TBF AVENGER

The portly Grumman Avenger was one of the most effective carrier-based aircraft of the war, despite a disastrous combat debut at the Battle of Midway, when all but one of those dispatched against the Japanese fleet were shot down. The XTBF-1 flew on August 7, 1941, and the initial production TBF-1 entered service in early 1942. With the F4F Wildcat and F6F Hellcat fighters competing with the Avenger for Grumman's factory space, production was subcontracted to General Motors' Eastern Aircraft Division, which built the type as the TBM, supplying over 75 percent of the nearly 10,000 built. Here a gaggle of TBF-1 Avengers set out on an early 1944 mission in the South Pacific. US national insignia evolved during the war. The red central spot was removed in May 1942 to avoid confusion with the Japanese hinomaru marking. Bars on either side were added to further differentiate the insignia in June 1943, initially with red borders. The return of red was not universally popular and, two months later, the borders were ordered to be overpainted in blue, although not all units complied at the same time. Soon after this photo was taken, the four-tone camouflage was replaced by overall sea blue, but Avengers in these colors were seen until the end of the war.

DOUGLAS SBD DAUNTLESS

A Douglas SBD Dauntless is craned aboard USS *Saratoga* at Pearl Harbor in June 1942. Following the Battle of Midway, which saw many Navy and Marine Corps aircraft destroyed defending the strategic islands, USS *Saratoga* ferried replacements to the squadrons at Midway. The white stripe on the fin of the aircraft helped the landing signal officer (LSO) on the flight deck judge if the SBD's landing attitude was correct. Originating in a design by Jack Northrop and refined by Edward Heinemann, the SBD-1 Dauntless first flew in early 1939. Just one example of the prewar fashion for dive-bombers, the "Slow But Deadly" SBD had large, perforated air brakes under the wings to slow it during the attack dive, and carried a 1,600lb (726kg) bomb in a swing-out cradle under the fuselage. Two 250lb (114kg) bombs could be mounted on the wings. Its career highlights were the battles of Coral Sea and Midway, but it also saw some action in Norway and North Africa, and with land-based US Marine Corps units. The US Army Air Force also used it as the A-24 Banshee. By 1943, the aircraft was considered obsolete by the US Navy, but was used in the Pacific from 1944 by New Zealand, and postwar by France, Chile, and Mexico. The most numerous variant was the SBD-5, with 2,965 built.

CURTISS SB2C HELLDIVER

The SB2C Helldiver was designed as a successor to the aging but worthy SBD Dauntless dive-bomber, although it never totally supplanted it. The XSB2C-1 prototype flew on December 18, 1940, and exhibited poor handling and stability and bad stall characteristics. Numerous small changes were made before deliveries began in December 1942, although it was not until November 1943 that it saw action. The Helldiver suffered from structural weaknesses and the aircraft broke up pulling out of dives and after hard carrier landings. Sensibly, the Royal Navy and US Army Air Forces rejected the Helldiver, but the US Navy committed to mass production from three factories, two of them in Canada. A total of 1,112 SB2C-3 models, like the one seen here, with a four-bladed propeller and a 1,900hp (1,397kW) Pratt & Whitney R-2600-20 engine, were produced. Bombs could be carried under the wings or in an internal bomb bay, and two 20mm (0.787in) cannon were fitted in the wings. The SB2C slowly proved its worth as a bomber. It had to, as a staggering total of over 7,100 were built, making it the most numerous dive-bomber ever. Some remained in service after the war and the type was later supplied to the French Navy and Hellenic Air Force, both of which used them in combat.

NORTHROP N3-PB NOMAD

An aircraft from California that never served with the US forces and mainly operated in Iceland, the Northrop N3-PB Nomad was built to a Norwegian specification. In early 1940, a Royal Norwegian Air Force purchasing commission toured US manufacturers seeking a replacement for its obsolete Marinens Flyvebaatfabrikk M.F.11 biplane patrol aircraft. Northrop offered a floatplane design based on its Model 8-A land-based light bomber. In early April, an order was placed for 24 aircraft, but Germany invaded a few days later and, after a hard-fought campaign, Norway came under Nazi occupation in June. Some of the many Norwegian airmen who escaped to Britain and joined the RAF were sent to Canada for training. From there, they went to Iceland and formed No. 330 (Norwegian) Squadron on April 25, 1941. The Nomads started arriving in May and the squadron began operations with flights based at Reykjavík, Búðareyri, and Akureyri. The N3-PBs flew anti-submarine patrols, air ambulance, and transport missions. Powered by a 1,200hp (890kW) Wright R-1820, the Nomad was armed with four forward-facing 0.50in (12.7mm) machine guns and two defensive 0.30in (7.7mm) guns. It could carry up to 2,000lb (907kg) of torpedoes, depth charges, or bombs.

VOUGHT OS2U KINGFISHER

The US Navy's requirement for a replacement for its Vought O3U Corsair observation biplane was met by the same company's OS2U Kingfisher, which first flew in March 1938. Initial trials were in landplane configuration with a fixed undercarriage, following which the prototype was converted to a floatplane. Launched from a catapult and recovered by crane, the Kingfisher became the principal scouting aircraft aboard US battleships and cruisers and was also used for inshore patrols operating from lagoons, lakes, and other sheltered waters. Able to carry light bombs underwing and fitted with two forward-firing 0.30in (7.7mm) machine guns, the Kingfisher was used for anti-submarine patrol, gunnery spotting, utility, and search and rescue missions. This OS2U-3 was assigned to heavy cruiser USS *Baltimore* (CA-68). Radioman/gunner Reuben Hickman is reaching for a cable, which he will attach to the aircraft so that it can be hoisted aboard, observed by pilot Denver Baxter, and rescued Hellcat pilot George Blair in the rear cockpit. Blair, from VF-9 on *Essex* (CV-9) had been shot down during a dawn fighter sweep over the Japanese base at Truk in the Caroline Islands on February 18, 1944, and floated in the lagoon under Japanese fire until picked up by the Kingfisher. Baxter was awarded the Distinguished Flying Cross for the rescue mission.

MARTIN PBM MARINER

Overshadowed by the Consolidated Catalina, of which twice as many were built, the Martin Mariner completed its maiden flight in February 1939, but required some redesign of the hull and tail before entering service in late 1940. Powered by two 1,900hp (1,417kW) Wright R-2600 Cyclone engines, the Mariner had less range than the Catalina, but could carry more. Its gull wings kept the engines out of the water spray. Rockets could be fitted to the fuselage sides to get it airborne at heavy weights. Armament usually included six 0.50in (12.7mm) machine guns in turrets and two more in the waist positions. Up to 2,000lb (907kg) of bombs or depth charges could be carried in bays in the engine nacelles. Above the cockpit on this PBM-5 is an AN/APS-15 surface search radar, which helped the Mariner find surfaced submarines and other targets. PBM squadrons destroyed a dozen U-boats in the Atlantic and several Japanese submarines in the Pacific during the war. The amphibious PBM-5A was the final postwar development. Production of the Mariner continued into 1949, and the aircraft served into the 1950s with the US Navy and Coast Guard, and with the Dutch, Argentine, and Uruguayan navies, the latter retiring the type in 1963.

MARTIN JRM-2 MARS

The Martin Mars was the largest flying boat of the war, first flown in June 1942. The original concept was for a patrol bomber like the company's earlier Mariner, but the role soon changed to transport, and the five production JRM-1s lost the twin tail and gun turrets of the XPB2M-1 prototype. The JRM-1 was powered by four 2,300hp (1,716kW) Wright R-3350-8 engines. All were named for Pacific island chains and were mainly used for moving cargo and personnel between California and the Pacific bases. *Caroline Mars* was the only JRM-2, which was built with 3,000hp (2,240kW) Pratt & Whitney R-4360-4 Wasp Majors. Its maximum take-off weight was 176,000lb (79,832kg) and, in February 1949, it set a record for passengers carried when it lifted 218 people from NAS North Island, San Diego, to NAS Alameda on San Francisco Bay. This was broken by *Marshall Mars*, which flew 308 passengers and crew on the same route two months later. The surviving JRM-1s were later re-engined with Wasp Majors and redesignated JRM-3s. The fleet was sold to a Canadian company, which used them for fire-bombing. *Caroline Mars* was destroyed in 1962 by Typhoon Frida, which blew it across Vancouver Airport. Two Mars remained in use as firefighters into the 2000s.

VOUGHT V-173

Encouraged by NACA, Charles Zimmerman convinced his employer, Vought Aircraft, to build a proof-of-concept aircraft based on his "discoidal" wing theories. The V-173 was flown on November 23, 1942, by Boone Tarleton Guyton. Because of its shape, it was nicknamed the "Flapjack" and "Flying Pancake," and was responsible for a number of "flying saucer" reports around NAS Patuxent River, Maryland, where it was tested. The airflow from the huge three-bladed propellers washed over the whole wingspan, providing a large amount of lift while avoiding wing tip drag. Despite its very small 80hp (60kW) Continental A-80 engines and fixed landing gear, the V-173 proved relatively fast at 138mph (222km/h). It could also fly very slowly and land in short distances, showing the potential of a larger version. The Navy funded construction of two larger XF5U-1 prototypes with Pratt & Whitney R-2800 radials buried in the wing roots. These drove four-bladed propellers via a complicated transmission system. The first XF5U-1 underwent extensive ground testing, but by 1944, the Navy was looking at jets for its future fighters and abandoned the project before it was flown. Both XF5U-1s were scrapped, but the sole V-173 was saved for the National Air and Space Museum collection.

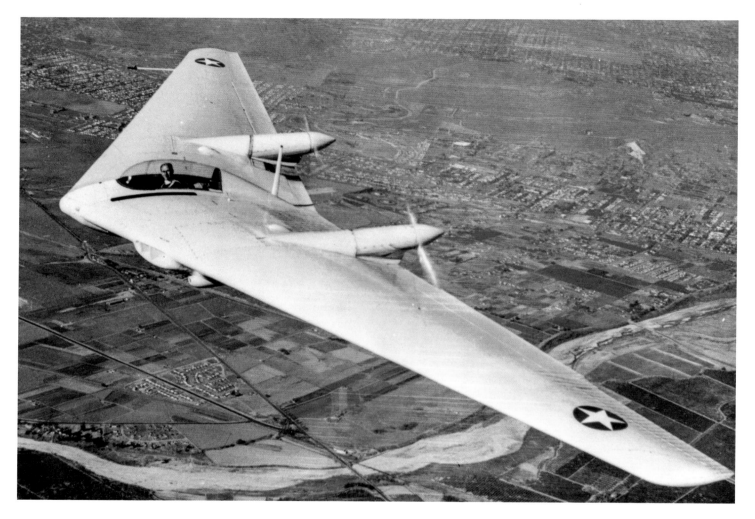

NORTHROP N-9M

Jack Northrop's N-1M flew in July 1940 and proved the all-wing concept, which would culminate in the B-2A Spirit stealth bomber nearly four decades later. Four larger N-9Ms were built as test aircraft for the B-35 flying wing bomber project. They were slightly over one-third the size of the proposed bomber, but largely made of wood. The N-9M employed two Mensasco C6S-4 Buccaneer inline piston engines, giving 275hp (205kW) each. Each drove a two-blade pusher propeller. Because of the low drag and light weight, these small engines gave the N-9M a top speed of 257mph (415km/h). The first example flew in December 1942 but crashed in testing and was replaced by the N9M-B, with 300hp (224kW) Franklin XO-540-7 engines. One of the first two N-9Ms, which were overall yellow, is seen over the Rio Honde east of Los Angeles in the hands of test pilot John Myers. The third aircraft was blue on top with yellow undersides and the N9M-B had those colors reversed. The N9M-B was restored to flight at Chino, California, in 1994 and spent many years on the airshow circuit. Sadly, it was lost in a fatal accident in April 2019.

CHAPTER 8

WINGS FOR PEACE

INTRODUCTION

The defeat of the Axis powers brought new opportunities – and concerns – for the American aviation industry. Although many were troubled by the loss of the huge contracts for warplanes, it was hoped this would be balanced by demand for new commercial and private aircraft.

Many companies began designing new civil aircraft long before the war ended. It was hoped that peace would herald a boom in private aviation, that those that fought in the skies would want to continue to fly after leaving the military services. Many did, but others never wanted to board an aircraft again. Although sales of light aircraft were brisk soon after the conflict, within a few years it was clear that the expected postwar boom in private aviation was not going to happen. Compounding the issue was the availability of thousands of former military trainers at a fraction of the price of a new sports aircraft. Many smaller firms found the going too tough and went out of business. Some of those that survived went on to become household names – Cessna and Piper remain synonymous with light aircraft to this day.

The same problems faced those offering new airliners. The United States was in a good position to re-equip the world's flag carriers with a new generation of airliners at the end of the war, having developed several suitable types as wartime transports. The prime examples were the Douglas DC-4 and Lockheed Constellation, but sales were limited by relatively high purchase costs and competition from less capable, but far cheaper, surplus military transports. Chief among the latter were variants of the Douglas C-47 – the prewar DC-3 – which served as the workhorse of many airlines postwar. Attempts to create a replacement for the famous "Gooney Bird" would occupy the minds of the designers of many manufacturers, with varying degrees of success, for many decades.

HUGHES H-4 HERCULES

More familiarly known as the "Spruce Goose" – although primarily constructed of birch – the Hughes H-4 Hercules flying boat became one of the world's most famous aircraft. This is despite the facts that only the prototype was built, it flew only once, and never entered service. It remains the largest flying boat ever built and had the greatest wingspan of any aircraft until the Scaled Composites 351 Stratolaunch Carrier was rolled out at the end of May 2017. The Hercules was conceived by Henry John Kaiser and built by the Hughes Aircraft Company – the original HK-1 designation denoting Hughes and Kaiser – as a strategic transport to bridge the Atlantic, making use of unrestricted materials. The expected payload was up to 750 troops or 150,000lb (68,040lb) of freight. Development began in 1942, with three expected to be completed within two years. Kaiser later withdrew from the project and Hughes continued with the redesignated H-4, but the project suffered significant delays. The prototype (NX37602) was built outside Los Angeles in California, but was only completed after the war ended, by which time its intended role had disappeared. It was transported to Long Beach for erection. A flight crew of 22, with Howard Hughes at the controls and Dave Grant as his copilot, flew the Hercules on November 2, 1947, during what was initially planned to be the third taxi test of that day. A further ten press and industry representatives were onboard for the 26 second flight. Although the Hercules was maintained in airworthy condition until Hughes passed away in 1976, it never flew again. Between 1980 and 1992, it was displayed alongside the ocean liner *Queen Mary* at Long Beach, before going to the Evergreen Aviation & Space Museum in McMinnville in Oregon.

LOCKHEED L-049 CONSTELLATION

One of the most elegant airliners ever produced, the Lockheed Constellation was also blessed with high speed, reliable performance, good operating economics and great passenger appeal. It was also available at the right time, having been flown and tested by the US Army Air Forces as the C-69 at the end of the war. Lockheed L-049-051 G-AHEN was the 20th Constellation built, originally expected to be delivered to the United States Army Air Forces as a C-69. It was delivered to BOAC on May 29, 1946, one of an initial five acquired by the flag carrier to fly its North Atlantic route. The airliner was given the name *Baltimore* and flew with BOAC until written off overshooting Filton outside Bristol on January 8, 1951, during a training flight. The airframe was then sold to Mel Adams & Associates and shipped to the United States, where it was rebuilt by Lockheed Air Services International at Idlewild, New York, using parts of a salvaged C-69. Re-registered as N74192, Lockheed sold the airliner to the charter operator California Hawaii Airlines, which flew tourists to Hawaii. In September 1953, the Constellation was acquired by El Al as 4X-AKD, the Israeli airline configuring it to carry 63 passengers, plus cargo. El Al withdrew the aircraft by 1961, but the following year, it again became G-AHEN for Euravia (London), arriving at Luton Airport on April 12, 1962. The Constellation was modified as L-049D with higher take-off and landing weights, while the airline changed its name to Britannia Airways on August 16, 1964. It retired G-AHEN in April the next year and it was broken up at Luton in the following months.

DOUGLAS DC-6

From the outside, the Douglas DC-6 looked like a simple stretch of the DC-4/C-54. Several important changes made it much better suited for long-range commercial operations, however, not least of which was the introduction of a pressurized cabin and more powerful engines. What became the DC-6 started as the XC-112 for the US Army Air Forces, which first flew on February 15, 1946, with Benjamin Odell Howard at the controls. By then, the war was over and military interest in the project was waning. Douglas soon recognized the potential of the aircraft to compete with the Lockheed Constellation airliner and the initial commercial DC-6 variant flew on July 7, 1946. Four main versions were produced: the DC-6, DC-6A with cargo door, DC-6B passenger aircraft, and DC-6C with provision for both freight and seating. Renewed US military interest was triggered by the Korean War, resulting in orders for the aircraft as the C-118 for the US Air Force and R6D for the Navy, both of which were known as the Liftmaster. A total of 704 were built between 1946 and 1958. DC-6 N90744 *Flagship Nevada* was delivered to American Airlines on November 24, 1947, remaining with the carrier for just under two decades, later being renamed *Flagship Roanoke*. It was last operated by Ecuatoriana of Ecuador in the first half of the 1970s, after it had been converted as a DC-6F freighter.

BOEING 377 STRATOCRUISER

Clipper America was the first of 21 Boeing 377-10-26 Stratocruisers delivered to Pan American World Airways, the launch customer for the airliner. When the order for 20 was placed on November 28, 1945, it was cited as the largest contract for commercial aircraft, with a value of US$25 million. Building upon the work undertaken on the military Boeing 367 Stratofreighter (C-97), it was originally expected that the Stratocruiser could be in service by the end of 1946, but the certification process was protracted and Pan Am was eventually able to put the aircraft into service in 1949. After it was rolled out on October 8, 1948, N1025V flew on December 4 and was delivered on January 31, 1949, initially undertaking route proving flights from San Francisco to Honolulu. Pan Am also later received the original prototype 377-10-19 (upgraded as a -26), plus the eight 377-10-29s delivered to American Overseas Airlines when it acquired the carrier. N1025V was later renamed *Clipper Rainbow* and then *Clipper Celestial* until withdrawn by the airline and placed into store at San Francisco in 1961. It was acquired by Israel the following year and converted at Lod by Israel Aircraft Industries as a freighter with a swing-tail. The aircraft was operated by the Israel Defense Force/Air Force as 4X-FPW/015, named *Beitar*, from May 1965 for a decade.

MARTIN 2-0-2

Like many manufacturers across the globe, the Glenn L. Martin Company worked on a design aimed at replacing the Douglas DC-3 postwar. Its contender was the Martin 2-0-2, a 40-passenger, twin piston-engined airliner with a tricycle landing gear, that offered a 100mph (161km/h) speed advantage over the DC-3. This helped Martin garner significant interest for the 2-0-2, including from Eastern Air Lines (50), Colonial Airlines (20), Pennsylvania Central Airlines (35), Northwest Airlines (40), Trans World Airlines (12), and United Air Lines (50), as well as Delta, Braniff, and LAN of Chile. Orville Edwin "Pat" Tibbs was at the controls of the prototype for its first flight on November 23, 1946, while the second (NX93002) flew on January 27, 1947, and the airliner was approved for airline service on August 13. Northwest Airlines became the initial operator, with ten ready for scheduled service by November 1947, by which time Martin held orders for around 155 2-0-2s. On August 28, 1948, a Northwest aircraft lost a wing, and 37 people were killed in the resulting crash. The cause was quickly traced to metal fatigue in a major wing spar, resulting in the grounding of the fleet while Martin looked at ways of making the 2-0-2 safe. Remedial modifications were made to the second prototype, which were later introduced to some existing and new-build aircraft as Martin 2-0-2As. The legacy of the accident, coupled with significant delays to deliveries, was the cancellation of most of the orders, resulting in only 47 2-0-2s being built. Martin instead developed an improved version, the 4-0-4, which combined the pressurized cabin of the one-off Martin 3-0-3 with a redesigned, safe wing. Once again, NX93002 was modified as the prototype, after which it was re-registered as N40400. It was withdrawn from use in 1950 and went to Piedmont as a source of spares.

STINSON 108 VOYAGER

As wartime production of the L-5 Sentinel tailed off, Stinson Aircraft of Wayne, Michigan, began to look at introducing a new Voyager for the postwar civil market, the Model 108. Retaining the same basic layout of the high-wing taildragger, the four-seater was announced in August 1945, initially powered by a 125hp (93kW) Lycoming engine as the Voyager 125. The performance was not entirely satisfactory but was improved by substituting the original powerplant for a 150hp (112kW) Franklin 6A4-150 to create the Voyager 150. Voyager 150 NC97742 was the fourth production aircraft. It was later converted as the prototype 108-1, which introduced an external baggage door and was offered from 1947, along with the Flying Station Wagon, an optional utility interior applicable to any variant. Further development created the 108-2, with a higher take-off weight and Franklin 6A4-165-B3 or -B5 of 165hp (123kW), which was marketed as the Voyager 165 and entered production from May 1948. The final version built by Stinson was the 108-3, with slightly more fuel and higher weights, plus a taller tail to maintain directional stability. By July 1948, Stinson had delivered 5,000 Model 108s, making it the best-selling American four-seater of the postwar period. Convair, the parent company of Stinson, was having second thoughts about the light aircraft market, however, and on November 29, 1948, it sold Stinson and its assets to the Piper Aircraft Corporation. Piper built a further 125 as Piper-Stinsons into mid-1949 on top of the 5,135 produced by Stinson. The very last Voyager was a single Model 108-5 built by Univair in the mid-1960s.

COMMONWEALTH SKYRANGER 185

Rearwin Aircraft & Engines was formed in Kansas City, Kansas, in April 1928. The last of its designs to enter production was the Skyranger, created as a replacement for the more expensive Rearwin Cloudster. The prototype of the side-by-side taildragger first flew on April 9, 1940, as the Model 165 Ranger, its Continental engine's horsepower indicated by the last two digits in the designation. Production moved on to the more-powerful Model 175 Skyranger certified in August 1941, aimed at the executive or sportsman pilot. It was joined on the market in October 1941 by the 180 and 180F (F for Franklin 4AC engine) and, in January 1942, by the 190F. Production ceased in 1942, by which time more than 80 examples had been built, with Rae Rearwin selling his company to a group of New York-based investors that October. On January 7, 1943, the company was reorganized as the Commonwealth Aircraft Corp., which built assault gliders for the US Army Air Forces during the war. Skyranger production restarted after the conflict, initially at Kansas City and then at Long Island, New York, standardizing on the Model 185 powered by the Continental C-85-12, which received its new type certificate on December 2, 1946. Only around 275 additional Skyrangers were built, however, including NC62901 seen over Jamaica Bay, New York. Commonwealth's fate was sealed by labor troubles, which combined with the postwar slump in light aircraft sales to force production to end in October 1946.

LUSCOMBE 8 SILVAIRE

The Luscombe Silvaire family started with the Luscombe 50, a prototype of which first flew on December 17, 1937. The aircraft was certified as the Model 8 on November 8, 1938, and five variants were developed as tourers and trainers before the United States entered the war. More powerful engines in the subsequent versions raised horsepower from the original 50hp (37kW) in the Model 8, to 75hp (56kW) in the 8C, with 65hp (48kW) units in the 8A, B and D. Around 1,112 production Luscombe 8 to 8Ds were built between 1938 and 1942 by the Luscombe Aircraft Development Corp. at Merver Airport, New Jersey, before the company concentrated on building components for other, military aircraft. Ownership passed from the founder, Donald A. Luscombe, at this point, as it became a government-operated facility. In 1945, production of the Model 8 recommenced at a new facility in Texas, Dallas, the name of the company changing to the Luscombe Airplane Corp. Improvements incorporated into the new Model 8 included metal clad wings with a single (rather than dual) bracing strut, while the 8E Silvaire Deluxe had an 85hp (63kW) Continental C-85 and squarer tail profile. Silvaire Deluxe NC2478K received its certificate of airworthiness in June 1948, going to Gordon H. Mims of Fort Worth, Texas. Its registration was canceled on June 7, 1949. The 8E was followed in 1948 by the 90hp (67kW) C-90-powered 8F, which also introduced flaps into the design. In the spring of 1949, Luscombe Airplane ceased trading and its assets were purchased by Temco Engineering, which continued production of the Silvaire under the Luscombe name into 1950. In 1955, all rights were sold to the Silvaire Aircraft Co. of Fort Collins, Colorado, which built the last 8Fs between 1958 and 1960. In total, around 5,867 of all variants were produced.

ERCO ERCOUPE 415

Many light aircraft designed and built before the United States entered the war were returned to production to meet an expected boom in flying postwar. A good example is the ERCO Ercoupe, which was put back into production not twice, but four times, by five companies over 30 years! The Ercoupe dispensed with rudder pedals, which were linked instead to a steering wheel-type control column. This made it incapable of being spun or side-slipped. Designed by Fred Weick for the Engineering and Research Corp (ERCO) of College Park Airport at Riverdale, Maryland, 112 Ercoupe 415-Cs were originally built in 1940–41. Production resumed in 1946. Ercoupe NC93315 (c/n 638) was a 1946 model 415-C, with a Continental C75-12 75hp (56kW) engine instead of the 65hp (48kW) A65-8 fitted in the original aircraft, greater design speeds, revised brakes, control system and windshield, and was assembled using new manufacturing processes. It was one of 4,311 415-Cs built by ERCO from a total of 5,081 of all variants produced by the company through to 1950. Forney Aircraft Company of Fort Collins, Colorado, put the aircraft back into production in 1958, building 138 of five F-1 Forney variants, with Air Products Co. of New Mexico building a further 25 the following year. Alon Inc. of McPherson, Kansas, resumed production in 1965, assembling 244 as A2-A Alons, while from 1968, Mooney Aircraft of Kerrville, Texas, built 52 A2-A Alons and 59 M-10 Cadets.

NORTH AMERICAN NAVION

It was assumed that pilots trained for military service during the war would want to continue to fly after the end of hostilities. Many companies hoped to cash-in on the expected postwar boom in sports aviation; North American's plans centered upon the NAvion, designed by the team under the leadership of Edgar Schmued, earlier responsible for the P-51 Mustang fighter. Its name came from the abbreviated form of North American Aviation used on the stock markets. The NAvion was a four-seater with a tricycle landing gear sturdy enough for off-field operations. North American announced the first flight of the prototype NA-143 (NX18928) in February 1946, selling the aircraft sometime after; it was last noted in 1952 at an airport in the Florida Keys. The production version was the NA-145, which had thicker metal skin – allegedly to consume surplus wartime stocks – and was introduced in mid-1946. North American built 1,027 NA-145s, plus 83 NA-154s as L-17As for the US Army, at Mines Field in Los Angeles, making a loss on each one it delivered. Production ceased on April 14, 1947, by which time North American still had around 300 NAvions awaiting customers, but in July, the rights to the program were bought by Ryan Aeronautical of San Diego, California. The first Ryan-built Navion (the company dropped the capital 'A') was delivered in October 1947 and the company produced 1,238 by May 1951, including 163 L-17Bs and three XL-22As for the US Army.

BEECHCRAFT 35 BONANZA

The "V" or butterfly tail made the Beechcraft 35 Bonanza one of the most recognizable American light aircraft of the postwar period. Beechcraft 35 Bonanza NX80040 was the second flying prototype, although the fourth built, as the initial pair were static test airframes. It was powered by a Continental E185 six-cylinder engine of 165hp (123kW), rather than the 125hp (93kW) Lycoming O-290-A of the first. The aircraft was later modified with wing tip and cabin fuel tanks and named *Waikiki Beech* by former US Army Air Forces Captain William Paul "Bill" Odom, who used it to set several distance records – all completed while wearing a business suit. On January 12, 1949, he flew from Honolulu, Hawaii, to Oakland, California, to set a light-plane distance record of 2,406.87 miles (3,873.48km) in 22 hours 6 minutes. The Bonanza was also used to capture a Fédération Aéronautique Internationale world record for distance in a straight line of 4,957.24 miles (7,977.92km), flying between Honolulu and Teterborough in New Jersey on March 7 and 8, 1949. Odom was airborne for 36 hours and 1 minute, the longest nonstop solo flight, with the Bonanza consuming 272.25 US gallons (1,036.6 liters) of fuel. He later flew the aircraft around the United States on a publicity tour for Beech Aircraft, before it went to the Smithsonian's National Air Museum. It was returned to Beech in 1951 and lent to Illinoi Congressman Peter F. Mack, who renamed it *Friendship Flame*, for a flight around the world. Mack left Springfield, Illinois, on October 7, 1951, returning there on January 27, 1952, after visiting 45 cities in 31 countries. It was later returned to the Smithsonian.

GOODYEAR GA-2 DUCK

Famous for building the FG variant of the Vought F4U Corsair during the war, the Goodyear Aircraft Corporation of Akron, Ohio, began work on a light amphibian in 1944, which first flew that September. The prototype, designated the GA-1 and named Duck, was a two-seater powered by a Franklin 4ACG-100-H3 piston engine of 107hp (80kW). It was conceived to evaluate new production techniques for potential postwar light aircraft, using all-metal construction except for partial fabric coverings on the wing and tail surfaces, and molded wood veneer and plastic for the wing tip floats. Goodyear went on to build additional aircraft with the same basic layout as the GA-2 Duck, which had a wider landing gear to improve ground handling, plus changes to the cockpit. Two passengers could accompany the pilot in the GA-2, which was powered by the 145hp (108kW) Franklin 6A4-145-A3 engine. The first flew in early 1946 and a type certificate was granted on February 28, 1947, while 15 more were produced (including NC5506M). The final six GA-2s built in 1949 were fitted with -165-B3s of 165hp (123kW) as GA-2Bs. Goodyear loaned out the aircraft to selected companies in the United States to gain operational experience of their structure, systems, and components, as it was these aspects the company planned to market, rather than the aircraft itself. The final variant, which appeared by 1950, was the GA-22 Drake with a revised hull, a larger variant that could carry four people. It was offered to the US military as a utility aircraft but failed to secure an order. The airframe was later rebuilt as the GA-22A with a 225hp (168kW) Continental E225-8 engine, first flying as such on March 18, 1953. It is the sole survivor of the Goodyear Duck family.

GRUMMAN G-58B "RED SHIP"

Only two Grumman F8F Bearcats were not produced for the US Navy. The second (N700A) was assembled from spare parts as a Grumman-owned demonstrator, known as the G-58B "Red Ship." The aircraft combined the airframe of the F8F-2 series with the 2,100hp (1,566kW) Pratt & Whitney R2800-34W Double Wasp powerplant of the F8F-1. It was first flown on January 1, 1950, and was used by the company's technical service and head of the sales division, Roger Wolfe Kahn (seen in the cockpit) to travel between the bases housing Bearcats (and other Grumman types) in the United States. In 1959, the aircraft passed to the Cornell Aeronautical Laboratories in Buffalo, New York. Successive private owners in Illinois and Louisiana owed N700A from 1966 until at least 1977. Between 1981 and 1984, it was displayed at the Champlin Fighter Museum at Mesa, Arizona, before going to Planes of Fame East at Eden Prairie, Minnesota, in 1986. In 1998, the G-58B went to the Palm Springs Air Museum in California, where it remains today in airworthy condition painted in US Navy colors that were applied around 2001 as *Bob's Bear*. The first civilian Bearcat was the G-58A *Gulfhawk 4*, built for the Gulf Oil Co. for Major Alford Williams. First flown on July 23, 1947, it was lost in a landing accident at New Bern, North Carolina, on January 1, 1949.

HILLER XH-44 HILLERCOPTER

At the age of 18, Stanley Hiller, Jr. designed and flew the first successful coaxial rotorcraft in the US. Flight trials of the XH-44 Hillercopter began on July 4, 1944, inside the Memorial Stadium on the Berkeley Campus of the University of California, where Hiller was a student. The aircraft had been built in a repair garage with a 90hp (67kW) Franklin engine, de-rated to 65hp (48kW), exchanged later for a 125hp (93kW) Lycoming. Using a coaxial rotor system enabled one set of blades to counteract the torque effect of the other, eliminating the need for a tail rotor. This saved weight and complexity (although introduced some of both), but mostly enabled all the engine power to be used to provide lift. With the financial help of shipbuilder Henry Kaiser, the XH-44 was developed into the two-seat X2-235, which had a metal fuselage and very rigid rotors as a safeguard against the two sets clashing during maneuvering flight. Hiller hoped to sell the design to the Navy, but it only took one uncompleted example for wind tunnel testing under the designation UH-1X. Two more X2-235s were built and got as far as tethered trials before Kaiser declined to fund production. Hiller's company subsequently designed other helicopters using the coaxial principle but was more successful with conventional designs such as the UH-12. The XH-44 is preserved in the National Air and Space Museum Collection.

BELL 30

Helicopter pioneer Arthur M. Young and his assistant, Bartram Kelley, arrived at Bell Aircraft in November 1941 to build and test prototypes of his design powered by a 160hp (119kW) Franklin engine. The first Bell 30, named *Genevieve*, was rolled out on December 24, 1942, and five days later, Young completed the first tethered flight at an altitude of 5ft (1.5m) at Cheektowaga (Gardenville) in New York, followed later that day by Floyd Carlson. In early January 1943, *Genevieve* was damaged in a crash, with pilot Bob Stanley badly injured, and it was not until June 26, 1943, following repairs, that Carlson completed the first untethered flight. The second Bell 30 (NX41868) featured a redesigned mounting for the tail rotor, new landing gear, a semi-monocoque fuselage, and an enclosed cockpit featuring "car-type" doors for the pilot and a passenger. It replaced *Genevieve* in the test program in late September 1943, the initial aircraft having suffered another crash that grounded it over six months for rebuilding. The second Bell 30 made its public debut in March 1944 and, on May 10, it was flown inside the 65th Regiment's armory at Buffalo in New York by Carlson, in front of an audience of Civil Air Patrol pilots and cadets. One of the Bell 30s was used to rescue a pilot who had bailed out of a Bell P-59 Airacomet near Lockport in New York state on January 5, 1945, while on March 14, two fishermen were rescued on Lake Erie. A third Bell 30, with an open cockpit, first flew on April 25, 1945. The idea of covering the cockpit with a Plexiglas "bubble" came from Young, a feature that became closely associated with the later Bell 47.

CHAPTER 9

PREPARING FOR THE COLD WAR

INTRODUCTION

In the five years following the war, American air power underwent significant changes, as a new generation of combat aircraft was developed to take advantage of new technology. It also witnessed the creation of an independent air force.

The formal surrender of Japan on September 2, 1945, ended the most destructive war ever fought. At the end of the war, the US Army Air Forces was the world's largest air arm with nearly 63,700 aircraft in service, while the US Navy and Marine Corps had approximately 41,000. The tremendous leaps forward in technology developed by the end of the conflict – jet engines, advances in aerodynamics, and the destructive power of the atom bomb – promised to revolutionize air combat and make existing types obsolete.

The pivotal role played by air power during the war gave weight to those calling for the creation of an independent air force. On July 26, 1947, the National Security Act was signed into law, with most of the changes coming into force on September 18. The Act established the US Air Force as a separate service from the Army Air Forces, under the Department of the Air Force, part of the National Military Establishment. Offensive and defensive air power was assigned to Strategic, Air Defense, and Tactical Air Commands, while Air Transport Command provided an airlift capability across the globe.

By mid-1950, the US Air Force had a total active inventory of 12,300 aircraft. The declining relationship between the Capitalist West and Communist East, highlighted by the start of the Korean War in June 1950, prompted a massive build-up of American military forces. Many of the aircraft developed in the immediate postwar years would go on to play a major role in the Cold War.

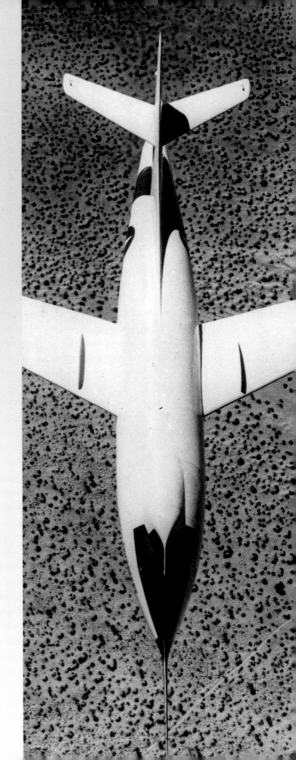

DOUGLAS XBT2D-1 DAUNTLESS II

One of many successful designs for Douglas by Edward Henry Heinemann, the AD (later A-1) Skyraider was developed as the XBT2D-1 Dauntless II to meet a shifting US Navy requirement from 1943. The designation was in the Bomber-Torpedo (BT) category, later simplified to A for Attack. It competed with the Martin XBTM-1 Mauler, which was ordered in small numbers, and the Curtiss XBTC-1, which was not. Company test pilot LaVerne Ward Browne conducted the XBT2D's maiden flight on March 18, 1945, and is seen at the controls of the first prototype, BuNo 9085, during the test program. The logo of the Douglas Testing Division is worn on the cowling, which covered a 2,300hp (1,692kW) Wright R3350-8 Cyclone. There were no fewer than 25 XBT2D-1s built out of a total of 3,180 Skyraiders. There were specialized airborne early warning and jamming variants with up to four crew members, as well as single-seat attack aircraft. Production ended in 1957 and A-1s served throughout the Korean and Vietnam wars, flying in the latter conflict with the US and South Vietnamese air forces, as well as the US Navy. With 15 weapons pylons and a pair of 20mm (0.787in) cannon, the rugged Skyraider was mostly used for close air support, although Navy A-1s shot down two Mikoyan-Gurevich MiG-17s in Vietnam.

LOCKHEED P-80 SHOOTING STAR

The P-80 was America's first operational jet. Legendary designer Clarence "Kelly" Johnson and his team had the first XP-80 (named *Lulu Belle*) ready in 143 days, and it flew at Muroc in California on January 8, 1944, with a 3,000lb (13.3kN) thrust de Havilland Goblin turbojet. Subsequent aircraft used the Allison J33-A-17, rated at 5,200lb (23.1kN). In early 1945, two of the 12 YP-80 service test aircraft were used for demonstration flights in England and two more were sent to Italy, where they were prepared for combat, although the European war had ended before that could take place. The initial production P-80A was very similar to the YP-80 but with the addition of dive brakes and modified intakes. The P-80B had minor changes over the P-80A. Water-alcohol tanks were fitted to give boost on take-off, although it reduced the fuel capacity. The Shooting Star was the first operational American warplane fitted with an ejection seat. The third P-80B, 45-8480, was issued to 56th Fighter Group before joining the Flight Test Department at Wright-Patterson AFB, Ohio. On June 5, 1948, the same month that the "P for Pursuit" was replaced by "F for Fighter" in the US Air Force designation system, it was written off at Muroc AFB.

NORTH AMERICAN XP-86 SABRE

North American test pilot George "Wheaties" Welch made the first flight of XP-86 45-59597 on October 1, 1947, and is depicted in the cockpit of the prototype during on an early test flight. At this time, the "buzz number" on the side began with "P for Pursuit," but changed to "F for Fighter" in 1948. The XP-86s were powered by a 3,820lb (17.0kN) Allison J35-C-3, but production F-86A Sabres used the General Electric J47-GE-2 of 5,000lb (22kN) thrust. Welch had shot down four Japanese aircraft over Pearl Harbor on December 7, 1941, and scored a total of 16 wartime victories in the Pacific. Before Chuck Yeager's official first supersonic flight on October 14, 1947, it is likely that Welch exceeded Mach 1 during test flights in the XP-86, but the aircraft was not then calibrated to measure airspeeds in the transonic regime. In 1949, the F-86 Sabre became the first swept-wing jet fighter to enter service and had a long career with the US Air Force and many other air arms, seeing air combat in Korea, and with Pakistan against India. The last examples were retired by Argentina in the mid-1980s. All three of the XP-86s were eventually destroyed in atomic weapons testing, with 45-59597 being subject to blasts in operations *Snapper Easy* and *Snapper Fox* at Frenchman Flat, Nevada, in May 1952.

REPUBLIC P-84 THUNDERJET

Republic, maker of the most-prolific American fighter, the P-47 Thunderbolt, produced its first jet fighter in 1946, with Major Wally Lien conducting the first flight of the XP-84 on February 28 at Muroc Army Air Field. The prototypes were powered by the General Electric J35-GE-7 turbojet, which gave 3,745lb (16.66kN) of thrust. These were followed by 15 YP-84A service test aircraft, of which 45-59488, seen here during 1947, was the fifth. These aircraft were used to familiarize pilots with the type before the production P-84B entered service. This example was later used by NACA, first at its Ames Aeronautical Laboratory at Moffett Field, California, then the High-Speed Flight Station at Edwards AFB, where it supplied parts to keep another YF-84 flying for research studies, pilot proficiency flights, and as a chase aircraft. The F-84 Thunderjet saw extensive use in Korea, mainly in the ground-attack role with six 0.50in (12.7mm) machine guns and up to 4,450lb (2,020kg) of bombs or rockets, and was later deployed in Europe armed with tactical nuclear weapons. The Thunderjet was followed by the swept-wing F-84F Thunderstreak fighter-bomber, and the RF-84F Thunderflash photoreconnaissance aircraft.

LOCKHEED XF-90

Designed by Clarence "Kelly" Johnson's team as a "penetration fighter" to escort bombers all the way to the target, the F-90 was to be armed with six 20mm (0.787in) cannon, mounted in threes under each intake. In configuration, the F-90 resembled a scaled-up F-80 Shooting Star with 35° swept wings and an innovative tailfin that moved together with the horizontal tailplane to adjust pitch. Tony LeVier flew the first of two XF-90s on June 6, 1949, and can be seen in the cockpit here. The first aircraft was fitted with two Westinghouse J34s of 3,400lb (15kN) thrust, and was seriously underpowered. Despite its sleek looks, it was outperformed in combat by the cheaper P-80, and as it was built with heavy-grade aluminum to withstand supersonic speeds, was much heavier than the rival McDonnell XF-88, which was selected to fulfill the requirement, but did not enter service. At the end of its flight test program, the XF-90A was transported to Frenchman Flats in the Nevada desert to study the effects of atomic weapons on modern airframes. Subjected to three blasts in 1952, the largely intact, but slightly radioactive, remains were recovered in 2002 and sent to the National Museum of the US Air Force at Dayton, Ohio.

GRUMMAN F7F TIGERCAT

When the Grumman XF7F-1 flew in December 1943, it embodied several novelties, going on to become the first production twin-engined carrier aircraft for the US Navy and the first with a tricycle undercarriage. During its service career, it infrequently operated from aircraft carriers, however, being primarily land-based with the Marines, which flew it in both day- and night-fighter roles. The aircraft had a maximum speed of 435mph (700km/h) and a range of 1,200 miles (1,931km). The largest of Grumman's wartime "Cats," the F7F was initially called the Tomcat, but this had changed to Tigercat by the time deliveries of the F7F-1 began in October 1944. The main production version was the single-seat F7F-3 (seen here), which had a taller fin and rudder and used Pratt & Whitney R-2800-34W Double Wasp radials. The Tigercat was just too late to see active service in the Pacific, but the F7F-3N and -4N night-fighter variants fought in Korea, where they scored victories against the biplane Polikarpov Po-2 used by the North Koreans as a "nuisance raider." Only the F7F-4N had an arrester hook for carrier operations. A total of 364 Tigercats had been built by the time production ended in late 1946. Some examples later had civilian careers as fire bombers, able to drop retardant on spots hard to reach by larger aircraft.

RYAN FR-1 FIREBALL

The US Navy was slower to introduce jet aircraft into service than the US Air Force, adopting the cautious approach of combining piston- and turbine-engine power in the same airframe. The Ryan XFR-1 Fireball took flight in July 1944 with a 1,425hp (1,048kW) Wright Cyclone in the nose and a 1,600lb (7.12kN) thrust Westinghouse J31 jet in the tail. Both engines would be used for take-off and during combat, with the piston engine alone operating during carrier landings. The high-speed dash capability would have been useful in combating kamikaze attacks, but the first Fireball squadron only formed in March 1945 and was not ready before the war ended. VF-66 deployed aboard USS *Ranger* (CV-4) in early May in order to qualify a core group of pilots for carrier operations but wrecked two of its three aircraft. In June, they tried again with more success, but the carrier was still preparing to deploy on operations when Japan surrendered. Two Fireballs of VF-66 are shown during the trials on *Ranger*, piloted by VF-66's commanding officer, Commander John F. Grey, and Lieutenant D. J. "Dixie" Mays. The FR-1 proved to be structurally weak and was outperformed by pure jets. Orders for 700 Fireballs were eventually canceled and only 66 were built. The last was retired in 1947 and only one has survived; it is on display at the Planes of Fame Museum in Chino, California.

McDONNELL FH-1 PHANTOM

McDonnell Aircraft of St. Louis, Missouri, had only built one original design, the XP-67 "Moonbat," before being awarded a contract for a carrier-based jet fighter in 1943. At one time, McDonnell considered six small (300lb/1.3kN thrust) engines, but settled for a pair of Westinghouse XB-2Bs rated at 1,165lb (5.2kN), later replaced by 1,600lb (7.1kN) J30s. For some reason the design was ordered with the designation XFD-1, D normally being allocated to Douglas' designs in the Navy's system. By the time production aircraft were being delivered in 1946, the more appropriate FH-1 designation was being used, as was the name Phantom, which appears here on one of the two XFD-1s, flying near St. Louis. On the first flight on January 26, 1945, one engine was replaced with ballast, as a second was not available. Westinghouse engines were famously underpowered and unreliable, but the FH-1 seems to have been an adequate fighter for its day, although orders were cut from 100 to 60. The Navy was satisfied enough to order a development of the same basic design and McDonnell duly completed the larger F2H Banshee in early 1947. It went on to see combat in Korea and was produced in night fighter and photoreconnaissance variants.

GRUMMAN F9F PANTHER

Grumman entered the jet age with the F9F Panther. The powerplant of choice was the 5,000lb (22.2kN) centrifugal flow Rolls-Royce Nene, license-built by Pratt & Whitney as the J42, but the US Navy hedged against underperformance by also ordering a prototype with the 4,600lb (20.5kN) Allison J33-A-8. This was installed in the third prototype, BuNo 122476 (seen here), which became the XF9F-3 and flew in August 1948 with Corwin "Corky" Meyer at the controls. The Navy ordered 47 J42-powered F9F-2s and 54 F9F-3s with J33s to evaluate their comparative performance and reliability. In the end, the J42 engine proved superior and the F9F-3s were re-engined with that powerplant. Most Panthers were F9F-5 variants with yet another engine, the 6,250lb (27.8kN) Pratt & Whitney J48, derived from the Rolls-Royce Tay. The F9F went on to be the most successful first-generation navy jet fighter and saw extensive action in Korea. Although mostly used for ground attack, it destroyed a small number of North Korean Mikoyan-Gurevich MiG-15s in air combat, but its inferior turning performance led to the development of the swept-wing F9F-8 Cougar. Both the Panther and Cougar were also used by the Navy's aerial demonstration team, the Blue Angels.

NORTH AMERICAN B-45 TORNADO

The B-45 Tornado was built to a November 1944 requirement for a jet bomber, which also spawned the Convair XB-46, Boeing XB-47, and Martin XB-48. North American's entry was aerodynamically conservative, with straight wings and four Allison J35 engines in paired pods on each wing. Its crew of four included a tail gunner armed with twin 0.50in (12.7mm) machine guns. The first of three XB-45s flew on March 17, 1947, at Muroc (later renamed Edwards AFB), California, and the B-45A entered service in February 1948. Some originally had J35s, but the majority were powered by General Electric J47s, which were later retrofitted to all B-45s. With a strengthened airframe and more fuel capacity, the first B-45C (48-001, seen here) flew on May 3, 1949. It suffered a structural failure at Edwards AFB in September 1950 but was repaired and used as part of the US atomic testing program. On November 1, 1951, it became the first jet aircraft to drop a nuclear bomb, during Operation *Buster-Jangle*. Six months later, it dropped another as part of Operation *Tumbler-Snapper*. It reportedly crashed in December 1952. Only ten B-45Cs were delivered to the USAF, but the model served as the basis for the RB-45C, which performed important Cold War reconnaissance missions.

MCDONNELL XHRH-1 WHIRLAWAY

McDonnell Aircraft bought the controlling share in the Platt-LePage Aircraft Company in 1944, which had worked on several helicopter projects. It had bought the rights to the Focke-Wulf Fw 61, which had twin rotors in a lateral configuration, and copied the configuration for the first helicopter accepted by the US Army, the Platt-LePage XR-1. The Navy asked McDonnell to scale up the design to accommodate eight people. The XHJD-1 Whirlaway flew on April 27, 1946, and it was quickly found to suffer from yaw instability, an inherent issue with lateral rotors. A horizontal tailplane with elevators was added and the XHJD-1 (later designated XHRH-1) proved able to lift heavy loads and reach considerable altitudes. One engine powered each rotor, but a novel transmission system enabled both to be driven in the event of engine failure. The large stub wings, on which the Pratt & Whitney R-985 engines, rotors, and landing gear were mounted, contributed to lift in forward flight. The Navy preferred the Piasecki XHRP-X, a tandem rotor design with a central engine, however, and only one Whirlaway, BuNo 44318, was built. After flying with the company until June 1951, it was donated to the Smithsonian Institution and remained in storage in mid-2022.

HUGHES XF-11

In 1942–43, the Hughes Aircraft Company, owned and directed by the increasingly eccentric tycoon Howard Hughes, constructed a twin-boomed fighter, the D-2, in great secrecy. The D-2 only made a few short flights and was destroyed in a hangar fire in late 1944, but much from the design later found its way into the XF-11, which was offered for the US Army Air Forces' requirement for a long-range, high-altitude reconnaissance aircraft. One difference was that the XF-11 was of conventional metal construction, rather than the compressed wood Duramold used on the D-2. Two Pratt & Whitney R-4360-31 Wasp Major radials driving eight-bladed Hamilton Standard contra-rotating propellers provided the XF-11's motive force. The XF-11's maiden flight, made on July 7, 1946, by Hughes himself, was a disaster. After an hour airborne, the starboard propeller pitch controls failed, and the aircraft became almost impossible to control. Hughes tried to crash-land on a country club golf course in Beverley Hills in Los Angeles, but hit three houses, destroying one. Hughes was badly injured and spent months in hospital. He recovered to fly the second prototype, 44-70156, with simpler Curtiss-Wright propellers, on April 5, 1947. By then, however, the US Army Air Forces had canceled orders for 100 F-11s and, after some testing in Florida, the second aircraft was used as a maintenance trainer in Texas before being scrapped.

NORTHROP F-15 REPORTER

The anticipated invasion of Japan in late 1945 called for extensive photographic coverage and thus a fast aircraft able to evade enemy defenses and return with the pictures in time to be of use to tactical commanders. The latest version of the Black Widow night fighter, the XP-61E, was modified to take a battery of cameras in the nose. A new fuselage housed the crew of two under a large Plexiglas canopy. On July 3, 1945, 42-8335 flew again as the XF-15 Reporter, "F" denoting "Foto" at the time, rather than "Fighter." The Reporter was powered by two Pratt & Whitney R-2800s of 2,100hp (1,600kW) each, giving it a top speed of 440mph (708km/h) at 33,000ft (10,058m). After the atomic bombings in August, the war ended before the Reporter could enter service and an order for 175 aircraft was reduced to 36 F-15As, the last of which was delivered in April 1947. At the same time, the one operational squadron to field the type began receiving aircraft to survey occupied Japan to aid in the country's postwar reconstruction. They also carried out an extensive photo survey of the Korean Peninsula, which proved extremely useful when the North invaded in June 1950.

FAIRCHILD XNQ-1

In 1945, the US Navy sought to replace its wartime primary and basic trainers with a single type. Three companies entered the competition: Beechcraft with the T-34 Mentor; Temco with the TE-1 (later the T-35 Buckaroo); and Fairchild with the XNQ-1, of which the first prototype (BuNo 75725, seen here) flew on October 7, 1946, at Hagerstown, Maryland. The XNQ-1 was a conventional all-metal design with a retractable landing gear. It had several engine changes during its life, starting with a 320hp (239kW) Lycoming R-680-13 radial, and ending with a 350hp (257kW) Lycoming GSO-580 eight-cylinder horizontally opposed powerplant. The Navy chose the Beechcraft T-34 to meet its requirements, partly for its tricycle undercarriage layout. The US Air Force also evaluated the three types, also choosing the T-34 in February 1949. The Fairchild entry (now named the T-31A) was rated second and the Temco came third. Nevertheless, an order for 100 T-31As was placed, but was later canceled in 1949. BuNo 75725 crashed in 1950, but the second prototype was kept at NAS Patuxent River in Maryland for student test pilots to fly and evaluate, before it passed on to the Civil Air Patrol. It was restored in 2002 and, two decades later, is flying as N5726.

NORTH AMERICAN T-28 TROJAN

North American Aviation, maker of the Texan used in great numbers by the US Air Force as the T-6 and the US Navy as the SNJ, scored another success with the T-28 Trojan basic trainer. This aircraft, 48-1371, was the first of the two XT-28 prototypes and made its maiden flight on September 24, 1949. The Air Force was impressed enough to order 266 T-28A Trojans in 1950 and eventually took delivery of 1,194 examples. With its frameless canopy, the Trojan had a greatly improved view for both the pilot and instructor and a tricycle undercarriage, which was a novelty for a trainer of the era, but eased the transition to jets. The T-28 was powered by an 800hp (597kW) Pratt & Whitney R-1830-1A radial engine. After an agreement to standardize initial training, the US Navy ordered 429 T-28Bs from May 1953 to replace the SNJ. The T-28B had a higher gross weight and a more powerful 1,425hp (1,062kW) Wright R-1820-86 engine. The T-28C added a tail hook for carrier operations. The first XT-28 was assigned to the Air Force Test Center at El Centro, California, and was designated a JT-28 in May 1956, signifying it was modified for temporary special testing. It was removed from the inventory in June 1965 and was last noted in one of the many scrapyards around Davis-Monthan AFB, Arizona.

TEMCO TE-1 BUCKAROO

The Buckaroo was a low-cost trainer version of the Globe GC-1B Swift, produced by the Temco Aircraft Corporation. Temco was formed by the Texas Engineering & Manufacturing Co. of Dallas, Texas, in 1947, after it acquired the rights to the Swift tourer. Initial interest in a trainer variant came from the Philippine Air Force, prompting Temco to produce a prototype TE-1A in late 1948 by modifying a Swift airframe. The aircraft was originally powered by a 125hp (93kW) Continental C-125 engine, which was quickly replaced by a 145hp (108kW) C-145-2H unit. In early 1949, the US Air Force began its search for a new basic/primary trainer, during which it evaluated a prototype TE-1A. Although the rival Beechcraft Model 45 (T-34) won, the US Air Force decided not to proceed with the program. Temco decided to redesign the TE-1A to military standards, with a new fuselage, a longer nose and raised rear decking, and a new center wing section. In late 1949, by which time the name Buckaroo had been selected, Temco was tooling up to build ten of the aircraft. Around the same time, a new US Air Force trainer competition was organized and three TE-1Bs were ordered by the service as YT-35s powered by the 165hp (123kW) Franklin 6A4-165-B3. Although it was again rejected, ten armed Buckaroos were later acquired by the US Air Force for supply to the Royal Saudi Air Force. Single examples of the TE-1A were also evaluated by the Israeli and Hellenic Air Forces.

BOEING XL-15 SCOUT

Boeing made a rare foray into light aircraft with the L-15 Scout, designed to operate in the liaison and battlefield observation roles. It featured a rear-facing observer's seat below the tailboom and full-span trailing-edge flaperons, which gave it a full-power stall speed of 18mph (30km/h). Cruise speed was 101mph (163km/h) with its 125hp (1,226kW) Lycoming O-290-7 engine. The landing wheels could be swapped for skis or floats, as illustrated here on the second XL-15, 46-521. It could be easily disassembled and towed behind a jeep. Developed by Boeing's Wichita division, the XL-15 first flew in July 1947. When the US Army Air Forces became a separate service in September 1947, the army was left with small aircraft and helicopters for liaison and light transport duties. A later agreement defined the maximum weights as 2,500lb (1,134kg) and 4,000lb (1,814kg), respectively. The Scout was near the limit at 2,216lb (1,005kg) fully loaded. Only two XL-15s and ten YL-15s were built. Orders for 47 L-15s were canceled and the aircraft were transferred to the US Fish and Wildlife Service in Alaska. Eventually, the service rationalized its fleet and the L-15s went onto the civil market. Having passed through several owners, as of mid-2022, 46-521 is stored in Minnesota as a potential restoration project.

BELL X-1

In the hands of test pilot Charles Elwood "Chuck" Yeager, the Bell X-1 made the first official flight beyond Mach 1, the speed of sound, on October 14, 1947. The X-1 was powered by a Reaction Motors XLR-11 rocket motor, which gave 6,000lb (27.0kN) thrust from four combustion chambers. The pilot's only engine control was the number of chambers fired. The X-1's shape was modeled on that of a 0.50in (12.7mm) caliber bullet, a shape known to easily go supersonic. The X-1 was carried aloft by a modified Boeing B-29 Superfortress bomber and dropped, unpowered, from 25,000ft (7,620m). On its record-breaking flight, Yeager ignited all rocket chambers and climbed to 42,000ft (12,801m), reaching 670mph (1,078km/h) before the five-minute supply of fuel ran out and he glided back to earth. Only one X-1 was built in the original configuration, but the X-1A, X-1B, and X-1E followed to further explore the flight envelope and reached speeds above Mach 2. Rocket propulsion proved effective at achieving high speeds for short periods but was never employed as the main propulsion source on an operational postwar fighter.

DOUGLAS D558-II SKYROCKET

The Douglas D558-II Skyrocket was the culmination of a joint program between the US Navy and NACA to explore high-speed flight. The first phase saw the D558-I Skystreak, a straight-winged jet, achieve several speed records during its 1947–53 flying career. Three swept-wing D558-IIs were built for supersonic research. The first was initially flown from Muroc Dry Lake, California, in conventional jet configuration by John Martin on December 10, 1947, powered by a Westinghouse J34. The original flush canopy was soon replaced by a raised one with a V-shaped windshield. An 8,000lb (35.6kN) Reaction Motors XLR-8-RM-5 rocket was installed in the summer of 1949, and Mach 1.0 was soon exceeded, but endurance was low. Two more D558-IIs were built and converted to all-rocket air-launched configuration, which saved the fuel otherwise used for take-off and climb. On November 20, 1953, Scott Crossfield piloted the Skystreak to 1,291mph (2,078km/h), becoming the first man to exceed twice the speed of sound. A follow-on project to achieve speeds of up to Mach 7 and altitudes of 189 miles (305km) was canceled in favor of pooling resources with the US Air Force on the North American X-15.

INDEX

People